Legalines®

Editorial Advisors:
Gloria A. Aluise
Attorney at Law
Jonathan Neville
Attorney at Law
Robert A. Wyler
Attorney at Law

Authors:
Gloria A. Aluise
Attorney at Law
Daniel O. Bernstine
Attorney at Law
Roy L. Brooks
Professor of Law
Scott M. Burbank
C.P.A.
Charles N. Carnes
Professor of Law
Paul S. Dempsey
Professor of Law
Jerome A. Hoffman
Professor of Law
Mark R. Lee
Professor of Law
Jonathan Neville
Attorney at Law
Laurence C. Nolan
Professor of Law
Arpiar Saunders
Attorney at Law
Robert A. Wyler
Attorney at Law

INCOME TAX

Adaptable to Fourteenth Edition* of Freeland Casebook

By Scott M. Burbank
C.P.A.

*If your casebook is a newer edition, go to www.gilbertlaw.com to see if a supplement is available for this title.

THOMSON

★

WEST

EDITORIAL OFFICE: 1 N. Dearborn Street, Suite 650, Chicago, IL 60602
REGIONAL OFFICES: Chicago, Dallas, Los Angeles, New York, Washington, D.C.

SERIES EDITOR
Linda C. Schneider, J.D.
Attorney at Law

PRODUCTION MANAGER
Elizabeth G. Duke

FIRST PRINTING—2007

Legalines®

**Features Detailed Briefs of Every Major Case,
Plus Summaries of the Black Letter Law**

Titles Available

Administrative Law ....Keyed to Breyer	Criminal Law ....Keyed to Dressler
Administrative Law ....Keyed to Schwartz	Criminal Law ....Keyed to Johnson
Administrative Law ....Keyed to Strauss	Criminal Law ....Keyed to Kadish
Antitrust ....Keyed to Areeda	Criminal Law ....Keyed to Kaplan
Antitrust ....Keyed to Pitofsky	Criminal Law ....Keyed to LaFave
Business Associations ....Keyed to Klein	Criminal Procedure ....Keyed to Kamisar
Civil Procedure ....Keyed to Friedenthal	Domestic Relations ....Keyed to Wadlington
Civil Procedure ....Keyed to Hazard	Estates & Trusts ....Keyed to Dobris
Civil Procedure ....Keyed to Yeazell	Evidence ....Keyed to Mueller
Conflict of Laws ....Keyed to Currie	Evidence ....Keyed to Waltz
Constitutional Law ....Keyed to Brest	Family Law ....Keyed to Areen
Constitutional Law ....Keyed to Choper	Income Tax ....Keyed to Freeland
Constitutional Law ....Keyed to Cohen	Income Tax ....Keyed to Klein
Constitutional Law ....Keyed to Rotunda	Labor Law.................................Keyed to Cox
Constitutional Law ....Keyed to Stone	Property ....Keyed to Cribbet
Constitutional Law ....Keyed to Sullivan	Property ....Keyed to Dukeminier
Contracts ....Keyed to Calamari	Property ....Keyed to Nelson
Contracts ....Keyed to Dawson	Property ....Keyed to Rabin
Contracts ....Keyed to Farnsworth	Remedies ....Keyed to Rendelman
Contracts ....Keyed to Fuller	Securities Regulation ....Keyed to Coffee
Contracts ....Keyed to Kessler	Torts ....Keyed to Dobbs
Contracts ....Keyed to Knapp	Torts ....Keyed to Epstein
Contracts ....Keyed to Murphy	Torts ....Keyed to Franklin
Corporations..............................Keyed to Choper	Torts ....Keyed to Henderson
Corporations..............................Keyed to Eisenberg	Torts ....Keyed to Prosser
Corporations..............................Keyed to Hamilton	Wills, Trusts & Estates ....Keyed to Dukeminier

All Titles Available at Your Law School Bookstore

THOMSON
™
WEST

SHORT SUMMARY OF CONTENTS

TABLE OF CONTENTS AND SHORT REVIEW OUTLINE

I. INTRODUCTION

A. TAX RATES

The tax tables and rate schedules used to compute the federal income tax are progressive; *i.e.,* the rate increases as taxable income increases.

1. **Individuals.** In the past, individuals were taxed under a structure characterized by many tax brackets and a large difference between the highest and lowest rates. The Tax Reform Act of 1986 reduced the number of tax brackets to two. The rate brackets were 15% and 28%. In 1991, a third tax bracket was added and two more brackets were added in 1993. The Economic Growth and Tax Relief Reconciliation Act of 2001 added yet another tax bracket and an overall reduction in the tax rates to be phased in over a number of years. For 2007, the six tax brackets are 10%, 15%, 25%, 28%, 33%, and 35%. Children under the age of 18 have to use their parents' marginal tax bracket on unearned income over $850. The new rates for married taxpayers filing jointly for 2007 are as follows:

Taxable Income	Rate
$ 0 to $ 15,650	10%
$ 15,650 to $ 63,700	15%
$ 63,700 to $128,500	25%
$128,500 to $195,850	28%
$195,850 to $349,700	33%
$349,700 and above	35%

2. **Corporations.** The tax rate structure for corporations is as follows:

Taxable Income	Rate
0 to $50,000	15%
$50,000 to $75,000	25%
$75,000 to $100,000	34%
$100,000 to $335,000	39%
$335,000 to $10,000,000	34%
$10,000,000 to $15,000,000	35%
$15,000,000 to $18,333,333	38%
$18,333,333 and above	35%

B. CONSTITUTIONAL HISTORY

1. **Pre-Sixteenth Amendment Years.** Before 1913, the federal government used the taxing power for the single purpose of raising revenues, particularly in time of war. The power to tax was limited by Article I, Section 9 of the

Constitution, which required that any ***direct*** tax be apportioned to the various states according to each state's population. The first income tax was held unconstitutional as an unapportioned direct tax in *Pollock v. Farmers' Loan & Trust Co.*, 157 U.S. 429 (1895). During that time taxes and tariffs on alcohol, tobacco, and real estate predominated.

2. **Sixteenth Amendment.** The Sixteenth Amendment took effect in 1913 and gave Congress the power to impose income taxes without regard to apportionment.

3. **Recent History.** Since 1913, the income tax has not been used solely as a device to collect revenue; revenue acts have been designed to stimulate capital formation, serve special interest groups, stabilize the economy, reduce deficits, and increase the "equity" in the system. These and other social objectives have resulted in the increased complexity and apparent inequity of the current tax system.

4. **Present Federal Tax Law.** Until the enactment of the Tax Reform Act of 1986, the statutory body of federal tax laws was referred to as the "Internal Revenue Code of 1954, as amended." However, because the 1986 amendments were so substantial, the current statute is now referred to as the "Internal Revenue Code of 1986."

C. SOURCES OF FEDERAL INCOME TAX LAW

Federal income tax law is based principally on statutes rather than common law.

1. **Internal Revenue Code of 1986 ("I.R.C.").** Title 26 of the United States Code ("U.S.C.") is the primary source of authority for federal tax law.

2. **Treasury Regulations.** Regulations are drafted by the United States Treasury Department under authority from Congress.

   a. **Legislative.** The regulations are drafted to cover specific provisions of the I.R.C. They carry the force of law unless they are drafted so broadly as to fall outside of their specific mandate.

   b. **Interpretative.** Some regulations are interpretative. These are issued under general authority granted by Congress, and are given a strong presumption of correctness by the courts.

3. **Revenue Rulings and Procedures.** Rulings and procedures are written by IRS attorneys and are not official pronouncements. They respond to a limited factual setting; accordingly, their scope is limited.

4. **Rulings and Determination Letters.** Letters of ruling or determination are written for taxpayers' inquiries sent to the IRS national office or a district director. These are issued only if a clear determination can be made from the

I.R.C., a treasury regulation, or a court decision. These letters cannot be cited as authority, but guide in determining the IRS position with regard to an issue.

5. **Judicial Opinions.** Tax controversies are heard by the United States Supreme Court, courts of appeals, district courts, and the United States Claims Court. In addition, the United States Tax Court is specifically set aside for tax issues.

D. INTRODUCTION TO INCOME TAX TERMINOLOGY

1. **Tax Computation.** The formula for computing individual income tax is as follows:

    Gross Income (I.R.C. section 61)
    >   Less: **Business Expense** (I.R.C. section 62)
    > =   **Adjusted Gross Income**
    >   Less: **Personal Exemptions**, and
    >   either the **Standard Deduction**
    >   or **Itemized Deductions**
    > =   **Taxable Income**
    >   Multiplied by **Tax Rate** (from the tables in
    >   I.R.C. section 1)
    > =   **Tax Due on Taxable Income**
    >   Less: **Credits**
    > =   **Tax Due**

2. **Capital Gain.** As will be shown later in this outline, capital gain or loss comes from the "sale or exchange of a capital asset." A capital asset is statutorily defined as "property," with a number of exceptions including inventory, property held by the taxpayer primarily for sale to customers in the ordinary course of a trade or business, and other limited exceptions. Until the Tax Reform Act of 1986, capital gains were taxed at a lower tax rate than other income. However, in 1987, the preferential treatment for capital gains was eliminated. The tax laws relating to the area of capital gains are numerous and complex. Most of this area of law is now relatively unimportant. However, Congress did not eliminate the need to distinguish between capital gain and ordinary income.

3. **Tax Accounting.** Normal accounting rules are followed generally for tax purposes. The two basic methods of tax accounting are the "cash receipts and disbursements" method (or "cash" method) and the "accrual" method. Under the cash method, amounts are treated as income when received in cash (or cash equivalents), and are deductible when paid. Under the accrual method, items are included in gross income when earned regardless of when payment is actually received, and items of expense are deducted when the

obligation to pay is incurred, regardless of when payment is made. Beginning in 1987, corporate taxpayers with gross receipts in excess of $5 million are no longer allowed to use the cash method of accounting.

4. **Realization and Recognition.** A gain or loss is said to be realized when there has been some change in circumstance such that the gain or loss might be taken into account for tax purposes. A gain realized is then said to be *recognized* when the change in circumstance is such that the gain or loss is actually taken into account. Therefore, a realization of gain does not necessarily bring forth immediate gain recognition. This is true in the case of asset appreciation.

   a. **Example.** If a capital asset is purchased for $20,000 and over the course of a five-year period it appreciates to $50,000, gain has been realized in the amount of $30,000. However, the gain will not be recognized until the asset is sold or otherwise disposed of.

5. **Depreciation and Cost Recovery.** Generally accepted accounting principles and basic tax accounting require the matching of expenses with revenues derived from such expenses. This "matching principle" precludes the current expensing of assets that benefit future periods.

   a. **Example.** Suppose a taxpayer purchases a machine that will produce inventory items that will be held for sale over a 20-year period. Even though the expense for the machinery has been realized or paid in the first year of operation, the matching principle requires that the cost of the machinery be spread over the 20-year period when revenues will be realized from its production. To recover this investment, the taxpayer takes a deduction traditionally called "depreciation." (Under the Economic Recovery Tax Act of 1981, Congress now terms depreciation as the Accelerated Cost Recovery System ("ACRS").) In any event, the principal idea is that the cost of the income-producing asset will be spread over its productive life. This will be explained in greater detail later in this outline.

6. **Entities.**

   a. **Proprietor.** A proprietor is a person who owns a business directly without partners or co-owners. All items of income and expense are treated as those of the proprietor herself.

   b. **Partnership.** A partnership is a combination of two or more people who have agreed to carry on a business for profit. Although the partnership files a tax return, it is a conduit for information purposes only, since items of income and expense flow through to the partners themselves.

   c. **Trust.** A trust is a device where a trustee holds and invests property for the benefit of another person. Generally, income and expenses of the trust flow through to the beneficiary. However, in some circumstances, the trust is required to pay the income taxes.

d. **Corporations.** Unlike a partnership, a corporation is treated as a separate entity from its owners. The corporation computes its income tax and makes a payment of tax on the net profit earned. Payments of income from the corporation to its shareholders are called "dividends." Dividends are taxed to the individual shareholders. In this regard, income is taxed twice when earned by a corporation. However, part of this double tax penalty is ameliorated by the generally low income tax rates charged to a corporation and the other tax advantages available to the corporation as an entity.

e. **S-Corporations.** An S-Corporation is a regular corporation formed under state law. However, for federal tax purposes, its shareholders are taxed in a manner similar to partners in a partnership. Note, however, that some states do not recognize this special tax treatment for purposes of state tax laws.

E. DEFERRAL AND ITS VALUE

It is generally understood that a dollar obtained today is worth more than what a dollar obtained in the future will be. This is due to the "time value of money" and is based on the notion that a dollar that is used today or invested is worth more than it could be when received in the future. The opposite is true for payments of expenses, such as income taxes. Thus, if a taxpayer can defer the payment of taxes, he obtains the interim benefit of using the taxes that would otherwise have been paid currently. For this reason, a common taxpayer strategy is not only the avoidance of tax, but also its deferral. Many transactions, such as like-kind exchanges (which will be discussed in greater detail, *infra*) are utilized solely for their deferral benefit. In fact, this concept is the basis of most legitimate tax shelters.

II. IDENTIFICATION OF TAX-ABLE INCOME

A. INTRODUCTION TO INCOME

1. **I.R.C. Doctrine.** I.R.C. section 61 defines gross income broadly as "all income from whatever source derived." Compensation for services, rents, royalties, interest, and dividends are explicitly included. Sections 71-87 mention additional items that are included. However, these are not considered exhaustive lists.

B. EQUIVOCAL RECEIPT OF FINANCIAL BENEFIT

1. **Found Money--**

Cesarini v. United States, 296 F. Supp. 3 (N.D. Ohio 1969).

Facts. The Cesarinis (Ps) purchased a used piano in 1957 at an auction for $15. In 1964, while cleaning the piano, they found $4,467 in old currency hidden inside. Ps declared that amount as ordinary income in 1964 and paid the tax on it. Later, Ps filed an amended return, which deleted the $4,467 as income and sought a refund of the tax paid, on the ground that found money is not ordinary income under I.R.C. section 61(a) and that even if it were income, it should have been declared in 1957, and thus recovery by the IRS (D) was barred by the three-year statute of limitations. Ps also argued that if the money was treated as income, Ps should receive capital gains treatment rather than being charged with ordinary income. The IRS denied the refund, and Ps appeal to the district court.

Issue. Must money that is found be declared as ordinary income?

Held. Yes. Appeal denied.

- ◆ I.R.C. section 61 specifically provides that "all income from whatever source derived" is to be included as income unless it falls under one of the I.R.C. exceptions. Found money is not one of those exceptions.

- ◆ Revenue Ruling 61, 1953-1 C.B. 17, specifically provides that "the finder of treasure trove is in receipt of taxable income . . . for the taxable year in which it is reduced to undisputed possession," and this position is reiterated in the Treasury Regulations. Because the money was not found until 1964, it is not income for 1957.

- ◆ Found money does not fit within the definition of a gift.

- Furthermore, this money is not entitled to capital gains treatment since found money is to be included as *ordinary* income in the year in which the taxpayer gains control over it.

---

2. Employer Paying Employee's Taxes--

Old Colony Trust Co. v. Commissioner, 279 U.S. 716 (1929).

Facts. American Woolen Company's board of directors voted to pay the income taxes due on the salaries of the main company officers, including its president, William Wood. Wood's taxes for the years 1919 and 1920 were $1,032,349.15, which the company paid in full. The Commissioner (P) argued that this amount was additional compensation to Wood, which must be included in Wood's taxable income. The Board of Tax Appeals upheld the Commissioner, and that decision is appealed to the courts.

Issue. Did the employer's payment of income taxes assessed against the employee constitute additional income to the employee?

Held. Yes. Judgment affirmed.

- The employer's payment of the tax was in consideration of the services rendered by the employee. Even though the payment was voluntary, it was not a gift. Presumably, the employee accepted this payment of his tax liability in lieu of some other form of compensation.

- Discharge of an obligation of the taxpayer by a third party is nevertheless a benefit (income) to the taxpayer.

- The form of payment makes no difference. It is therefore immaterial that the taxes were paid directly to the government.

Comment. Cash or property received as compensation for services is income, regardless of the form of payment. Other examples are a lessee paying the lessor's mortgage and a corporation paying an officer's fines.

---

3. Punitive Damages--

Commissioner v. Glenshaw Glass Co., 348 U.S. 426 (1955).

Facts. Glenshaw Glass Company (P) won a settlement from Hartford-Empire Company of $800,000, approximately $325,000 of which represented punitive damages for fraud and antitrust violations. Glenshaw did not report this portion of the settlement as income, and the Commissioner (D) assessed a deficiency. In a companion case, William Goldman Theatres won treble damages from Loew's, Inc. in the amount of $375,000 for antitrust violations. Of this, $125,000 was for actual lost profits and $250,000 was punitive. Goldman did not declare the $250,000 and D assessed a deficiency. Both cases present the same issue and were consolidated on appeal. In both cases, the Tax Court and the court of appeals upheld the taxpayers, who argued that the definition of income under I.R.C. section 22(a) (1939) did not include exemplary or punitive damages recovered in a lawsuit. The IRS argued that the damages were lost income under section 22(a).

Issue. Is money received as exemplary damages for fraud or as the punitive two-thirds portion of a treble-damage antitrust recovery reportable as gross income by the recipient under section 22(a)?

Held. Yes. Judgment reversed.

♦ Income is broadly defined as ". . . gains or profits and income derived from any source whatever." The Court has consistently interpreted this provision broadly to give Congress "the full measure of its taxing power." The money received is a windfall gain and increase in wealth to the recipient, and is not specifically exempted from income by any provision of the I.R.C.

♦ The money recovered that represents lost profits is clearly taxable as the profits would have been, had they been earned. By the same logic, the punitive damages are an increase in wealth from the same source and should be treated likewise, absent clear congressional intent to exempt them from income.

Comment. Section 22(a) corresponds to the current section 61(a). Also, in limited circumstances, I.R.C. section 186 allows a deduction to offset damages received in cases involving antitrust violations.

---

4. **Frequent Flyer Miles--**

Charley v. Commissioner, 91 F.3d 72 (9th Cir. 1996).

Facts. Dr. Charley (P) and his wife owned 50.255% of the shares of Truesdail Laboratories, a laboratory testing company. As an employee of the company, P traveled to various testing sites to inspect machinery. For such trips the company would bill the client for a round trip first class ticket. P would then instruct a travel agent to arrange for coach service to and from the site but charge the company for first class travel. The travel agent would then upgrade P's coach ticket to first class using P's frequent flyer miles. The travel agent then transferred funds to P's personal travel account for the difference between the coach price and the first class price charged to the company. The Commissioner (D) and the Tax Court held that the travel credits transferred to P's account constituted taxable income. P appeals.

Issue. Did the conversion of travel credits to cash result in taxable income reportable by P?

Held. Yes. Judgment affirmed.

♦ The credits can be characterized as additional compensation paid by the company to P.

♦ Alternatively, the frequent flyer miles belonged to P with a zero tax basis. Converting them into cash resulted in a taxable gain in the amount of cash received.

---

5. **Application of *Glenshaw*.** The Supreme Court in *Glenshaw Glass*, *supra*, attempted to define gross income as "undeniable accessions to wealth, clearly realized, and over which the taxpayers have complete dominion." This definition is much more inclusive than that of an earlier case, *Eisner v. Macomber*, 252 U.S. 189 (1920), which defined income as gains derived from capital and labor. Any increment in net worth is presumed to be income, unless it is specifically excluded.

   a. **Repayment of a loan.** A lender receives no income from a loan repayment. This is merely a change in the form of property from that of a receivable to cash. However, interest received on the loan is income.

   b. **Borrowing money.** Receiving a loan does not produce income since liabilities have increased along with assets, leaving net worth the same as before.

   c. **Noncash receipts.** Noncash receipts may be income even if the benefit is in the form of property or service.

   d. **Unsolicited property.** Unsolicited property, *e.g.,* property received in the mail, is not income unless there is an intent to retain the property or some associated benefit is shown.

   e. **Illegal increases in net worth.** Money or property that the taxpayer obtains through illegal activities is includable in his gross income because, as a practical matter, the criminal derives readily realizable economic value from it. The fact that the money really belongs to another is immaterial. Thus, proceeds from prostitution, extortion, embezzlement, and illegal gambling are all taxable.

6. **Unemployment Benefits.** Unemployment benefits that are paid to individuals pursuant to a federal or state program are fully taxable.

C. INCOME WITHOUT RECEIPT OF CASH OR PROPERTY

1. **Imputed Income--**

Helvering v. Independent Life Insurance Co., 292 U.S. 371 (1934)

Facts. Independent Life Insurance Company (P) owned an office building and used a portion of the building for its own offices. The IRS (D) took the position that the rental value of that space should be considered income by P. P brought suit alleging that this position violated Article I, Section 9, Clause 4 of the Constitution as a direct tax that must be apportioned.

Issue. Must a taxpayer declare as income the fair market rental value of a building that it owns and occupies?

Held. No. Judgment for P.

♦   This is a direct tax on the property that, under Article I, Section 9, Clause 4 of the Constitution, must be apportioned among the states. The rental value of a building used by the owner is not income under the Sixteenth Amendment.

Comment. Imputed income is created when a taxpayer works for or uses his property for his own benefit. If a taxpayer lives in his own house, he is theoretically paying himself rental income. Likewise, a homemaker receives imputed income for domestic services rendered in the home. While Congress is generally recognized as having the power to tax imputed income under the I.R.C., it has never attempted to do so. Such a tax would be an impossible administrative burden. In addition, most people do not think of imputed income as income, and this idea would meet severe political resistance.

---

2. **Barter Income.** In Revenue Ruling 79-24, 1979-1 C.B. 60, the IRS held that services exchanged by a lawyer and a housepainter are taxable income to each individual to the extent of the market value of the services. The IRS also held that the value of a work of art exchanged by an artist for rent on an apartment is taxable income to both the landlord and the artist.

3. **Use of Corporate Property**

Dean v. Commissioner, 187 F.2d 1019 (3d Cir. 1951).

Facts. The Deans (Ps) were the sole shareholders of a personal holding company. The corporation's assets included a home, which Mrs. Dean owned and contributed to the corporation in exchange for stock. Ps occupied the home as their residence, and Mrs. Dean expended a great deal of her personal funds in the upkeep and beautification of the property. The Commissioner (D) and the Tax Court held that the fair rental value of the residence should be included in Ps' gross income. Ps appeal.

Issue. Does free use of corporate property by its sole shareholders as their personal residence constitute gross income to them?

Held. Yes. Judgment affirmed.

◆　　It was the taxpayers' legal obligation to provide a family home. If it was done by occupying property that was held in the name of the corporation of which the taxpayers had control, the fair market value of that occupancy was income to them.

D. EXCLUSION OF GIFTS

1. **Rules of Inclusion and Exclusion.** Gross income includes any financial benefit received that is:

    a. Not a mere return of capital;

    b. Not accompanied by a contemporaneously acknowledged obligation to repay;

    c. Not excluded by a specific statutory provision; and

    d. Not within the concept of a tax-free fringe benefit.

2. **Gifts Defined--**

Commissioner v. Duberstein, 363 U.S. 278 (1960).

Facts. Duberstein referred customers to Berman, which proved to be profitable to Berman. Although Duberstein did not expect payment, Berman gave him a Cadillac. Berman then deducted the price of the car as a business expense. Duberstein did not include the Cadillac as income. The Commissioner asserted a deficiency, and the Tax

Court affirmed the Commissioner's determination. The court of appeals reversed. In a second case, Stanton was the controller of a church. When he resigned, the church's board voted him a "gratuity" of $20,000. Stanton had no enforceable right or claim to the payment. He did not include the $20,000 in his income. The Commissioner asserted a deficiency. After paying the deficiency and after administrative rejection of a refund claim, Stanton sued the United States for a refund. The district court held for Stanton, but the court of appeals reversed. The United States Supreme Court granted certiorari in both cases.

Issue. Were Duberstein's car and Stanton's money given to them with a "detached and disinterested generosity" so as to constitute gifts?

Held. No. Judgment in *Duberstein* reversed. Judgment in *Stanton* vacated and remanded to the district court.

♦ If payment is in return for services rendered, it is irrelevant that the donor derives no benefit from it. The payment is not a gift—it is income. Here, Duberstein and Stanton rendered services.

♦ The mere absence of a legal or moral duty to make such a payment, or the lack of economic incentive to do so, does not itself show a gift.

♦ Whether a transfer amounts to a gift depends upon consideration of all the facts surrounding the transfer. The trier-of-fact should be given discretion in determining the donor's intent.

Comment. A gift exists if it "proceeds from a detached and disinterested generosity, out of affection, respect, admiration, charity, or like impulses." The primary motive of the donor is determinative, and this definition is narrowly applied by the courts to restrict many would-be "gifts."

———————

3. **Employee Gifts.** In the past, many cases dealt with the issue of employees excluding payments made by their employers as gifts. Such cases typically involved a transfer of property or cash to an employee upon retirement, death, or in recognition of current outstanding service. The Tax Reform Act of 1986 made it clear that I.R.C. section 102 does not apply to employer-employee relationships. I.R.C. section 102(C) was added and provides that an employee "shall . . . not exclude from gross income any amount transferred by or for an employer to, or for the benefit of, an employee."

4. **Bargain Purchases.** Whether a taxpayer's purchase of property for a bargain price is a gift or income depends on the motive of the seller and all of the surrounding circumstances. For example, if an automobile dealer allows certain employees to purchase cars at below the market price as an employment

benefit, the bargain element is income to the employee. Here, the benefit is given as compensation rather than as a gift.

5. **Tips.** Tips and gratuities are income to the recipient.

E. EXCLUSION OF BEQUESTS

Gross income does ***not*** include property received by devise, bequest, or inheritance. [*See* I.R.C. §102(a)]

1. **Will Contest Settlement--**

Lyeth v. Hoey, 305 U.S. 188 (1938).

Facts. Lyeth's (P's) grandmother died, leaving most of her estate to a church. P and the other heirs contested the will, alleging undue influence. Before trial, a compromise was reached whereby the estate was split between the church and the heirs. The IRS (D) assessed a tax deficiency against P on the grounds that the money he received was pursuant to a contract, not inheritance. Massachusetts law supported D's viewpoint. The district court found for P, and the court of appeals reversed. P appeals.

Issue. Is money received in compromise of rights under a will contest to be characterized as taxable income?

Held. No. Judgment reversed.

♦ P obtained the money because of his standing as an heir and his claim in that capacity. If he had obtained the money by a judgment, it would have been exempt. The distinction between acquisition by judgment and acquisition by compromise in lieu of judgment is too formal to be sound because it ignores the heirship underlying the compromise.

♦ Estate taxes will be applied regardless of the will contest. Congress has not shown any intention to tax that property again as income when it is distributed to heirs.

♦ In addition, application of the federal exemption is not to be determined by varying local laws. The income tax laws should be interpreted so as to give a uniform nationwide application. Thus, money received in compromise of a claim as an heir is excluded under I.R.C. section 102 as property acquired "by gift, bequest, devise, or inheritance."

---

2. **Compensation for Past Services--**

Wolder v. Commissioner, 493 F.2d 608 (2d Cir. 1974).

Facts. Wolder (D), an attorney, contracted with a client, Marguerite Boyce, to provide lifetime legal services in exchange for a provision in her will to leave him securities. When the client died, D received $15,845 and 750 shares of common stock. D did not report the sum as income, and the IRS (P) assessed a tax deficiency. D argued that the bequest was exempt from income under I.R.C. section 102(a), which provides: "Gross income does not include the value of property acquired by gift, bequest, devise or inheritance." The Tax Court found the bequest taxable income under section 61. D appeals.

Issue. When a bequest is made to satisfy a contractual obligation, does it constitute taxable income to the recipient under section 61?

Held. Yes. Judgment affirmed.

◆ Whether a payment is a gift or compensation depends on the intent of the parties. In this case, a transfer in the form of a bequest was the method that the parties chose to compensate D for his legal services, and that transfer is therefore subject to taxation, whatever its label by federal or by local law may be.

Comment. The *Duberstein*, *supra*, "intent test" is used here. In this case, the defendant relied on *United States v. Merriam*, 263 U.S. 179 (1923), where a testator made cash bequests to his executors "in lieu of all compensation." The Supreme Court allowed the exclusion from income as a gift, stating that the executors were under no obligation to perform specific services but merely to make a good faith effort to be executors. Compare that result with the nature of the legal services rendered in *Wolder*.

F. EMPLOYEE BENEFITS

1. **Fringe Benefits.** Under the Tax Reform Act of 1984, some fringe benefits furnished by employers are specifically excludable, such as group term life insurance of up to $50,000 per year and accident and health insurance paid for by the employer. Congress has set forth rules for determining whether other fringe benefits should be excludable.

   a. **No-additional-cost service.** Employees may exclude a no-additional-cost service—a service provided to the employee that is regularly offered for sale to customers where the employer incurs no substantial additional cost (and forgoes no revenue) in providing the service.

   b. **Qualified employee discount.** A qualified employee discount allowing an employee to purchase a good or service routinely sold by the employer at a price equal to cost (for products) or at not more than a 20% discount (for services) is excludable by the employee.

c. **Working condition fringe benefit.** An employee may exclude a working condition fringe benefit, *i.e.,* any property or service provided to an employee that the employee could have deducted or depreciated if he had paid for the item himself.

d. **De minimis benefits excluded.** An employee may exclude any fringe benefit that is de minimis.

e. **Tuition reduction excluded.** An employee of an educational institution may exclude the value of tuition reduction at his institution (or a cooperating institution) for himself, his spouse, or a dependent child. This benefit does not apply to reductions at graduate schools.

2. **Meals and Lodging--**

Herbert G. Hatt v. Commissioner, 28 T.C.M. 1194 (1969).

Facts. Herbert G. Hatt (P) married Dorothy Echols, the president and majority shareholder of the Johann Corporation, which operates a funeral home. As part of an antenuptial agreement, Dorothy transferred 130 shares of Johann stock to P, and he became general manager of the funeral home and president and majority shareholder of the corporation. After the marriage, P moved into an apartment located in the funeral home building. P answered business calls in the apartment and, as was customary in the area, met with customers during nonbusiness hours. The Commissioner (D) assessed a deficiency against P, denying deductions for maintaining the apartment and claiming a constructive dividend to P for the fair rental value of the apartment.

Issue. May the value of employer-furnished lodging be excluded from gross income when the taxpayer controls the employer corporation?

Held. Yes. Judgment for P.

♦ I.R.C. section 119 grants an exclusion from gross income for the value of employer-furnished lodging if three conditions are met:

(i) The lodging is on the business premises of the employer;

(ii) The employee is required to accept such lodging as a condition of his employment; and

(iii) The lodging is furnished for the convenience of the employer.

♦ Although P's position enabled him to determine the "convenience" of the employer and the "conditions" of his own employment, this alone does not disqualify P from taking the exclusions or Johann from taking the deductions. Here, P is allowed to take the section 119 exclusion, since a showing was made that it was customary and necessary in that area that the manager of a funeral home reside on the premises to perform his duties. Although the ambulance drivers could take night calls, they were not authorized to carry on funeral business, especially financial aspects.

Comment. Although not at issue here, the "on the premises" test is of great importance in other cases. The term means either at a place where the employee performs a significant portion of his duties or where the employer conducts a significant portion of her business. Thus, the deduction was denied in *Commissioner v. Anderson*, 371 F.2d 59 (6th Cir. 1966), where a motel manager was "on call" at an employer-owned residence two blocks from the motel.

G. PRIZES AND AWARDS

1. **Test.** I.R.C. section 74(a) provides that "gross income includes amounts received as prizes and awards." Section 74(b) excludes a prize or award from income if (i) the prize or award was made in recognition of religious, charitable, scientific, educational, artistic, literary, or civic achievement; (ii) the recipient was selected without any action on his part to enter the contest; (iii) the recipient is not required to render future services as a condition of receiving the prize or award; and (iv) the prize or award is transferred directly to a governmental unit or to a charitable organization. Thus, if the recipient accepts the prize or award in his behalf, it is included in income.

2. **Business Trip--**

Allen J. McDonell, 26 T.C.M. 115 (1967).

Facts. Allen J. McDonell (P) was assistant sales manager for Dairy Equipment Company. The company held a contest and awarded a trip to Hawaii for its top 11 distributors and their wives. To prevent the trip from turning into a complaint session, the company decided to send a sales manager and his wife to "guide anticipated informal discussion" and otherwise protect the company's image and interests. P and his wife were chosen to go by lottery and were instructed to consider the trip as an assignment. P's wife was required to go because it was felt that single men could not host an outing for couples. P paid income tax on the value of his wife's trip. The IRS (D) determined a deficiency for the total value of the trip, asserting that the trip was either an award (taxable under I.R.C. section 74) or additional compensation, taxable under section 61. P seeks a refund in the Tax Court, asserting that the trip was required for both him and his wife by virtue of P's employment.

Issue. If an employee is required to go on a trip for business purposes, does the value of the trip represent taxable income to the employee?

Held. No. P is entitled to a refund.

♦ Business trips are not taxable compensation. There is no evidence of any intent on the part of the company to regard the trip as compensation. The company had sound business reasons (*i.e.,* to protect its image and interests) for requiring the trip. Thus, it was no different from any other business trip. Also, P's wife's duties could not have been performed by a single man.

♦ The mere fact that P was chosen by lottery does not make the trip an award or prize under section 74. P was not even a participant in the sales contest, and the right to go was unrelated to work performance.

♦ The trip was not a vacation, but a "command performance to work." It is significant that P and his wife never even got a chance to go swimming. The fact that the contest winners were on a vacation or that P and his wife enjoyed the trip is immaterial, since a legitimate business interest was being served.

H. SCHOLARSHIPS AND FELLOWSHIPS

1. **Prior Law.** Prior to the Tax Reform Act of 1986, amounts received for scholarships and fellowships were excluded from gross income. In addition, if degree candidates were required to perform services as a part of obtaining the scholarship (or fellowship), the income attributable to such services was taxable. However, if such services were required of all degree candidates, the entire scholarship was nontaxable.

2. **Changes in the Law.** The Tax Reform Act of 1986 modified prior law and allows only a limited exclusion, limited to degree candidates. In addition, the scholarship must be used for tuition, fees, books, supplies, or equipment required for specific courses. The new law retains the provisions related to the taxability of payments for services, but repeals the exception for services, required of all candidates.

3. **Employer Educational Assistance Programs.** I.R.C. section 127 provides for an exclusion for amounts received under a qualified educational assistance program. The maximum exclusion under this program is $5,250 and must be used for education-related costs. This exclusion is not available for graduate school level courses.

I. GAIN FROM DEALINGS IN PROPERTY

1. **Introduction.** Inherent in the concept of income is the notion of *net gain*. Thus, if A purchases stock for $100,000 and sells it for the same price, she has no income. For tax purposes, income equals the amount realized minus the adjusted basis of the taxpayer (*i.e.,* only net gain is taxed).

2. **Basis.** Generally, the "basis" of property is the cost thereof, including the cash or property given up to obtain the asset.

   a. **Cost as basis--**

Philadelphia Park Amusement Co. v. United States, 126 F. Supp. 184 (Ct. Cl. 1954).

Facts. Philadelphia Park Amusement Company (P) was granted a 50-year franchise to operate a passenger railroad to its amusement park. When the franchise was about to expire, P offered the city a bridge it had built for a cost of $381,000, in exchange for a continuation of its franchise. Several years later, when the renewed franchise still had several years to run, the railroad was abandoned in favor of bus service. P took depreciation deductions based on the cost of the franchise extension and a loss upon abandonment of the franchise. The IRS (D) denied the deduction and argued that since the bridge had no value, and since there had not been a taxable exchange, there had been no loss. P argued that the value of the franchise equaled the value of the bridge (its cost) and that the undepreciated basis could therefore be taken as a loss.

Issue. Is the basis of property (the franchise extension) the value of the property received in a taxable exchange?

Held. Yes. Judgment reversed and case remanded for proper valuation of the bridge and, if possible, the franchise.

♦ A transfer of assets is a taxable event unless exempted by statute. The taxpayer is taxed on the difference between the adjusted basis of the property given in exchange and the fair market value of the property received in exchange. Thus, the taxpayer's basis in the new property is its fair market value on the date of transfer.

♦ If, however, the fair market value of the new asset (the franchise) cannot be readily determined, the basis is the value of the asset (the bridge) given up in an arm's length transaction. Thus, P can take a loss on the undepreciated value of the franchise at the date of abandonment.

♦ The fact that P did not properly record the exchange does not prevent it from being a taxable event.

---

   b. **Expenses of acquisition.** Attorneys' and brokers' fees and the like spent in acquiring property are added to the cost basis.

   c. **Mortgages.** Cost also includes any purchase-money mortgage or trust deed on the property, whether or not the taxpayer is personally liable on the mortgage. It also includes any existing mortgage or trust deed that the taxpayer either assumes or takes subject to. [Crane v. Commissioner, *infra*]

d.   **Long-term debt.** The Tax Court has allowed a purchaser to include in his basis the entire debt when the purchase price of property of $300,000 involved $5,000 down, $5,000 to be paid in one year, and $290,000 to be paid in 99 years (*i.e.,* a total cost or basis of $300,000). But the courts will look to the circumstances of the transaction to determine whether the debtor is actually assuming the risks of ownership and a real obligation for the claimed cost basis.

e.   **Tax-detriment rule.** The cost basis includes any income charged to a taxpayer in acquiring property, such as a purchase below market value. For example, if a taxpayer pays $10 for stock in his employer's corporation that is really worth $25, the $15 difference is income. However, the $15 is also added to his "cost basis" in the stock, raising his basis in the stock to $25.

f.   **Property acquired by gift**.

1)   **Donee assumes donor's basis--**

Taft v. Bowers, 278 U.S. 470 (1929).

Facts. Taft (P) received a gift of appreciated stock from her father. She later sold the stock at a profit. She paid tax on the gain in value that occurred while she owned the stock, but did not pay on the amount the stock appreciated while held by her father. The IRS (D) assessed a deficiency on the ground that a donee assumes the donor's basis, as provided in section 202 of the Revenue Act of 1921 (now I.R.C. section 1015(a)). P argued that the basis should be the fair market value on the date of transfer. P also argued that Congress did not have the power to enact section 202; *i.e.,* P argued that an increase during the donor's ownership period cannot be assessable as income to the donee. The district court held for P, and the court of appeals affirmed.

Issue. Does a donee assume the donor's basis in property acquired by gift?

Held. Yes. Judgment reversed.

♦   A donor is exempt from income taxation if he makes a gift of property. Thus, if P's position were sustained, the amount of increase in value during the period the property was held by the donor would go untaxed. Congress intended to tax the gain derived from capital investments, and the provisions of section 202 are appropriate for enforcing a general scheme of lawful taxation.

Farid-Es-Sultaneh v. Commissioner, 160 F.2d 812 (2d Cir. 1947).

Facts. Taxpayer (P) and her future husband entered into a prenuptial agreement whereby she was to receive shares of stock in his company in return for her relinquishment of her rights to support and any inchoate interest in his property. His cost basis in the stock was $.16 per share. This would be P's basis if it were determined that she received the stock by gift. The stock had a value of $10.67 at the date of her acquisition. This would be the basis of the stock if her acquisition was not by way of gift, but for consideration. P sold the stock in 1938 and used the higher (fair market) value as her basis in computing her gain. The Commissioner (D), determining the acquisition to be a gift, assessed a deficiency, and P appealed. The Tax Court held for D, and P again appeals.

Issue. Did P receive the stock as a gift?

Held. No. Judgment reversed.

♦   No absolute gift was made since the transfer initially was contingent upon the death of the donor before marriage. When that event did not occur, the transfer was still made, but in consideration for P giving up other rights.

Comment. Had P lost, the basis of her stock would be the donor's basis (*i.e.,* $.16 per share). Since it was held not to be a gift, the basis is the value of the stock at the date of transfer (its fair market value). In the gift situation, for computing gain the donee takes the donor's basis. For computing loss, the donee's basis is the fair market value at the date of the gift or the donor's basis, whichever is lower.

---

g.   **Inherited property.** Under I.R.C. section 1014, a stepped-up basis for property passing by way of inheritance is permitted. Generally, the basis of the property becomes its fair market value at the time of the decedent's death. Thus, if the decedent owned property having a basis to him of $4,000 and a fair market value of $10,000 at the date of his death, the recipient of the property would have a basis of $10,000, which is a "step-up" of $6,000.

h.   **Property acquired between spouses or incident to divorce.** I.R.C. section 1041 provides that a gain or loss will not be recognized on a transfer of property from an individual to a spouse, or to a former spouse, provided that the transfer is merely incident to the divorce.

3.   **Amount Realized.** The "amount realized" is the total amount of money received in the transaction plus the fair market value of any property received in the transaction.

a. Money's worth received is the amount realized--

International Freighting Corporation, Inc. v. Commissioner, 135 F.2d 310 (2d Cir. 1943).

Facts. During the years 1933 through 1936, the International Freighting Corporation (P) adopted a stock bonus plan that awarded shares of stock to employees. Under the "class B" plan, employees would receive shares of stock if they contributed to P's success through their ability, efficiency, and/or loyalty. Recommendations for eligible employees were made by the president or department heads to the executive committee. P was under no obligation to regularly make the bonus payments, and paid varying amounts at the board's discretion. In 1936, P paid to the beneficiaries of its class B award 150 shares of Du Pont Company stock whose cost to P at the date of delivery was $16,153, with a market value at that time of $24,859. P claimed a deduction of the higher amount on its 1936 return. The Commissioner (D) reduced the deduction to $16,153, stating that the basis for calculation of the amount was the cost of such property rather than its fair market value. After P appealed to the Tax Court, D amended his argument, stating that P was entitled to the increased deduction, but that P realized a taxable profit of $8,705 on the disposition of the shares. The Tax Court held for D, and P appeals.

Issue. Is it possible for a corporation to realize taxable gain when it pays stock bonuses to employees?

Held. Yes. Judgment affirmed.

- The shares given in this case were not a gift by P, but were compensation for services actually rendered. Therefore, delivery of the shares constituted a disposition for a valid consideration. The consideration received by P was the work performed by the workers earning the stock bonuses.

- It is true that I.R.C. section 1001(b) provides that "the amount realized" is the sum of "any money received plus the fair market value of property (other than money) received." However, in circumstances such as these it has been held that "money's worth" is received and that such a receipt comes within the confines of the section. If there had been no formal bonus plan and P had simply paid the shares to selected employees as additional compensation, there would surely have been a taxable gain.

Comment. Note that in this case the corporation was able to claim the deduction in the amount of its basis in the stock. However, it was forced to declare as profit the gain of the difference between the fair market value and its basis in the stock. It follows that the employees received additional compensation of $24,859.

---

b.   Cancellation of indebtedness--

Crane v. Commissioner, 331 U.S. 1 (1947).

Facts. Crane (D) inherited an apartment building and land subject to a mortgage. The value of the property equaled the mortgage of $262,000, meaning that D's equity in the real estate was $0. D never assumed the mortgage on the property, and in 1938, she sold her interest for $3,000. After deducting selling expenses of $500, D claimed a capital gain of $2,500, stating that her adjusted basis in the property was her net equity of $0. In Tax Court, the Commissioner (P) argued that the property acquired and sold was the physical property itself, undiminished by the mortgage. Thus, the IRS position was that the basis was $262,042.50 minus $28,045.10 in allowable depreciation, equaling an adjusted basis of $233,997.40. The amount realized from sale included not only the cash received (or $2,500), but also the mortgage subject to which the property was sold (or $255,000). The Tax Court held for D. The court of appeals reversed, and D appeals.

Issue. Is the basis equal to the net value of the property less the unassumed mortgage?

Held. No. Judgment affirmed.

♦   A mortgagor not personally liable on the debt who sells the property subject to a mortgage and for other consideration realizes a benefit equal to the amount of the mortgage as well as the additional consideration received.

♦   "Property" is the physical thing that is the subject of ownership, or the sum of the owner's rights to control and dispose of the property.

♦   Depreciation deductions are based on the value of the property. If D's reasoning were used, the depreciation deductions taken on the property would have resulted in a negative basis in the property or have been disallowed altogether.

Dissent (Jackson, J.). D was never personally liable for the debt and hence was relieved of no debt upon sale of the property.

Comment. The transaction is treated as if the transferor had sold the asset for cash equivalent to the amount of the debt and had applied the cash to the payment of the debt. In *Crane*, the Court stressed the need to include the mortgage in order that the definition of "property" be the same for acquisition, depreciation, and disposition. Had D's basis been zero, she could not have taken a depreciation.

c.   Mortgage balance exceeds value of property sold--

Commissioner v. Tufts, 461 U.S. 300 (1983).

Facts. A partnership was formed with the purpose of building an apartment complex. Six days later, the partnership entered into an agreement with the Farm and Home Savings Association for a loan and mortgage of $1,851,500 to finance construction. Under the agreement, neither the partnership nor any of the partners (including Tufts (P)) assumed personal liability for repayment of the loan. After the complex was constructed, the partnership had difficulty renting the units and consequently had difficulty meeting its mortgage payments. Finally, two years after the loan agreement was signed, each partner's interest was sold to a third party (Bayles) for $250 in sales expense and assumption of the mortgage. The property's fair market value at that time was not more than $1.4 million. The Commissioner (D), stating that the partnership had realized the full amount of the nonrecourse obligation, assessed P his share of a $400,000 deficiency. The Tax Court held for D, but the court of appeals reversed. D appeals.

Issue. Does the *Crane* rule, *supra*, regarding nonrecourse mortgages, apply where the mortgage exceeds the value of the property disposed of?

Held. Yes. Judgment reversed.

♦ The *Crane* decision requires the amount of a nonrecourse liability to be included in the property's basis and the amount realized on its disposition. This is based on the assumption that the mortgage will be paid in full and represents an obligation to pay.

♦ Absence of personal liability on a mortgage does not relieve the borrower of his obligation to repay, but only limits the mortgagee's remedies on default. When a mortgage is assumed, the borrower is relieved of the obligation to repay monies received tax free.

Concurrence (O'Connor, J.). The logical way to view cases like this is to treat the ownership and sale of property separately from the loan and its retirement. The fair market value would be used as a basis of the property when acquired and sold. As for the assumption of a nonrecourse loan with a value less than the property disposed of, a classic cancellation of indebtedness (with gain recognition) would occur.

J. LIFE INSURANCE

Benefits paid on a life insurance policy by reason of the insured's death are not taxable under I.R.C. section 101, subject to the following exceptions:

1. **Installment Payments.** If the benefits are paid in installments rather than in a lump sum, the interest portion of the installments is income to the beneficiary.

2. **Cash Surrender Value.** If the insured elects to take the cash surrender value of the policy, that value might exceed his basis. In that case, he would have taxable income on the excess because it is not paid by reason of his death.

K. ANNUITIES

1. **Introduction.** An annuity contract is one in which the taxpayer invests a fixed sum, which is later paid back, with interest, in installments for a set period or for life. That part of each annuity payment that represents the taxpayer's investment in the policy is exempt as a return of capital. The interest portion, however, is income under I.R.C. section 72.

2. **Treatment.** Calculating the return of capital portion is done by determining the exclusion ratio. I.R.C. section 72(b) defines the exclusion ratio as the cost of the annuity divided by the expected return. The expected return is calculated by either a fixed contract or by reference to the life expectancy of the investor. The life expectancy is determined from actuarial tables. The amount excluded from each payment is the product of the exclusion ratio and the payment. The amount of each payment that exceeds this return-of-capital portion is then taxed as net income. Note that certain employee pension plans that work quite similarly to annuities are treated differently.

L. DISCHARGE OF INDEBTEDNESS

When a debtor obtains forgiveness of a debt absolutely or for a payment below the face amount of the debt, the extent of debt forgiven is income to the debtor.

1. **Forgiven Debt Is Income--**

United States v. Kirby Lumber Co., 284 U.S. 1 (1931).

Facts. Kirby Lumber Company (P) issued its own bonds for their face value of $12,126,800. During the same year, P repurchased some of the bonds at a discount of $137,521. The IRS (D) claimed that this was income (as a forgiveness of debt at a lesser amount than the actual debt) and assessed P accordingly. P paid the tax and brought suit for a refund.

Issue. Does retirement of a debt for less than face value represent income to the debtor?

Held. Yes. Judgment affirmed.

♦ Gross income includes "gains or profits" and income derived from any source whatever. If a corporation sells and then retires bonds at less than their face value, the excess is gain or income for the taxable year.

---

2. Exceptions.

    a.   **Insolvent debtors.** If a debtor was insolvent both before and after the debt cancellation, the gain realized by the debt cancellation is not income to him. He will recognize income, however, to the extent that the debt cancellation makes the debtor solvent. [I.R.C. §108]

    b.   **Gifts.** If a personal or family relationship is shown and the debt cancellation was intended as a gift, no income is recognized by the debtor.

    c.   **Contributions to capital.** A shareholder's forgiving a debt owed to him by his corporation is looked upon as a contribution to capital and is not income to the corporation.

    d.   **Compromises of disputed claims.** If a cancellation or reduction of debt is in reality a compromise of a disputed claim rather than a fixed debt, no income is recognized.

3. Contested Liability--

Zarin v. Commissioner, 916 F.2d 110 (3d Cir. 1990).

Facts. Zarin (P) was a compulsive gambler. During 1978 and 1979, P lost $2.5 million playing craps at a casino at which he had developed a $200,000 line of credit. The state Casino Control Commissioner issued an order making further extensions of credit to P illegal. During 1980, the casino increased P's credit line. P ran up a debt owed to the casino in the amount of $3,435,000. The casino filed a court action to collect the debt from P. P claimed that the debt was unenforceable due to regulations intended to protect compulsive gamblers. In 1981, the casino and P entered into an agreement to settle the debt for a total of $500,000. The Commissioner (D) determined a deficiency for P's 1980 return, claiming that P recognized $2,935,000 of income from the cancellation of the debt. The Tax Court held for D, and P appeals.

Issue. Does the settlement of a contested liability result in income from discharge of indebtedness?

Held. No. Judgment reversed.

♦   P owed an unenforceable debt to the casino of $3,435,000. After P disputed his obligation to pay the debt, both parties agreed to settle for $500,000. Given the circumstances regarding the enforceability of the debt, both parties agreed that the debt was not worth $3.4 million, but that it was worth something. The amount of the debt could not be determined until settlement. Therefore, P was deemed to have owed the casino $500,000, and since he paid the casino $500,000, no income to P was generated.

- Additionally, the I.R.C. section covering income from discharge of indebted-ness, I.R.C. section 108, does not apply since P was not liable for the unen-forceable debt, and P did not receive property subject to the debt.

Dissent. P received an entitlement worth $3.4 million, which would have been income except that he recognized an offsetting obligation to repay $3.4 million. If something that would otherwise be includable in gross income is received on credit in a purchase money transaction, there should be no recognition of income so long as the debtor continues to recognize an obligation to repay the debt. However, the income should be recognized when the debtor no longer recognizes an obligation to repay and the credi-tor has released the debt or acknowledged its unenforceability.

M. DAMAGES AND RELATED RECEIPTS

1. **Social Security and Workers' Compensation Benefits.** Social Security benefits for disability, workers' compensation benefits, and other forms of welfare benefits are excluded from gross income, including payments for work required of welfare recipients.

   a. **Old age benefits from Social Security.** Under I.R.C. section 86, old age benefits from Social Security (as opposed to disability benefits) are partially taxable depending on the amount of the taxpayer's adjusted gross income ("AGI") and the amount of benefits received. Up to 85% of Social Security benefits may be included as AGI exceeds certain levels.

2. **Business Injuries--**

Raytheon Production Corporation v. Commissioner, 144 F.2d 110 (1st Cir. 1944), *cert. denied*, 323 U.S. 779 (1944).

Facts. Raytheon Production Corporation (P) settled a lawsuit under the federal anti-trust laws against R.C.A. The allegations in the antitrust suit were that the illegal con-duct of R.C.A. completely destroyed P's business. The Commissioner (D) found that the settlement should have been included in P's gross income. P claimed that the settle-ment was not a recovery of lost profits, but a recovery of goodwill that was not taxable.

Issue. Is a settlement received for injury to goodwill taxed as income?

Held. No, subject to limitations.

- Compensatory damages from lost profits are taxable as income, but there is nothing here to indicate that P's suit was for recovery of lost profits.

♦ Damages given as reimbursement for lost capital, such as goodwill in P's settlement, are treated as a return of capital to the extent of basis. However, compensation for the loss of goodwill in excess of basis is gross income.

---

3. **Personal Injuries or Sickness.** Damages recovered, whether by judgment or settlement, because of personal injuries or sickness are specifically excluded by I.R.C. section 104(a)(2).

   a. **Background.** Even prior to the enactment of the statutory exclusion, such recoveries were held not income by rulings and judicial decisions. The rationale was that such damages, which are designed to make a person whole again, are like replacement of capital and hence are not income.

   b. **What constitutes "personal injuries."** Congress acted in 1996 to limit the exclusion from income to only cover damages incurred from physical injuries or physical sickness. Damages from nonphysical personal injuries are no longer excludable from gross income.

   c. **Punitive damages.** The 1996 act resolved the controversy surrounding the inclusion of punitive damages under Section 104(a)(2). Punitive damages are now specifically *included* within gross income.

4. **Future Payments for Personal Injury.** Revenue Ruling 79-313 involved a taxpayer who sustained permanent injuries after being struck by an automobile, for which he accepted a settlement from the driver's insurer. The insurer agreed to pay the taxpayer 50 consecutive annual payments, which would increase each year by 5% over the amount paid in the preceding year. The settlement agreement provided that the insurer was not required to set aside specific assets to secure the obligation. The question raised was whether the 50 consecutive payments were excludable from the taxpayer's taxable income. The IRS decided that they were, holding that all payments received pursuant to a settlement agreement for personal injuries are excludable from taxable income. If the taxpayer had received a lump sum payment, all future income generated from the settlement proceeds would be taxable. Thus, the form of the recovery appears to control.

5. **Accident and Health Insurance Benefits.**

   a. **General rule.** Benefit payments received under an insurance policy purchased by the taxpayer are excluded even if the taxpayer has already deducted the premiums for the policy.

   b. **Employer-carried plans.** If the employer pays for health and accident insurance for employees, the employees are not taxed on the premiums.

If the employer directly pays for medical expenses of employees or their dependents, they are not taxed on these payments. However, these payments must be made pursuant to a "plan for employees" adopted by the employer.

N. SEPARATION AND DIVORCE

1. Alimony and Separate Maintenance Payments.

a. Direct payments. Payments between spouses in connection with marital dissolutions are treated consistently between both parties. That which is taxable to the one spouse is deductible by the other. Conversely, a nontaxable receipt by one spouse is not deductible by the other.

b. Requirements for alimony to be taxable. I.R.C. section 71(b) lists various requirements that must be met in order for payments to qualify as deductible alimony. These include:

1) The payment is received by, or on behalf of, a spouse under a divorce or separation instrument;

2) The instrument does not designate the payment as a nonalimony payment;

3) In the case of a decree of legal separation or divorce, the parties are not members of the same household at the time of payment;

4) There is no liability to make any payment in cash or property after the death of the payee spouse;

5) The payment is not for child support; and

6) The payment must be in cash.

c. Excess front loading. Taxpayers are required to include in income "excess" alimony amounts paid during the first two years after the divorce. The "excess" amounts are determined as follows:

Year 1 payments less (average of year 2 and year 3 payments + $15,000)

Plus

Year 2 payments less (year 3 payments + $15,000)

The excess amount is included in income in year 3.

Section 71(f) requires that payments in excess of $10,000 must be made for six years after separation, barring death or remarriage of either spouse.

d. **Indirect payments.** If payments are made merely to maintain property owned by the payor spouse that is simply used by the payee spouse, they do not qualify as indirect alimony payments. These include premium payments on life insurance or mortgage payments on real property where the underlying property is owned by the payor spouse. However, if payments are made in satisfaction of a legal obligation exclusively that of the payee spouse and are applicable with respect to property in which the payor spouse has no legal interest, such indirect payments qualify as deductible alimony.

2. **Property Settlements.** Payments that fail to meet the section 71 criteria to qualify as alimony are either property settlements or child support. In either case, they have neutral tax consequences. That is, the payor spouse gets no deduction, and the payee spouse is not assessed taxable income. [I.R.C. §1041]

3. **Child Support.** Unlike alimony, payments made to an ex-spouse for child support are not entitled to a deduction. Taxpayers used to be able to draft divorce agreements to disguise payments for child support as alimony. In 1984, Congress enacted I.R.C. section 71(c)(2), which provides that any amount of payments pursuant to a divorce agreement that is reduced upon the happening of a contingency related to the child (*e.g.*, the child marries or becomes emancipated) shall be deemed child support no matter how the instrument describes the payments.

4. **Alimony Trusts.** As a general rule, trust income is taxable to the grantor when it is used for the support of any beneficiary whom the trustor is legally obligated to support. However, under I.R.C. section 682(a), a trust set up by a spouse, the income of which is paid to a divorced or separated spouse, is effective to shift the tax burden from the grantor to the beneficiary.

O. TAX-EXEMPT INTEREST

1. **Gain from Personal Residence.** Married individuals may exclude up to $500,000 of gain realized on the sale of a residence. Single individuals may exclude up to $250,000 of gain from the sale of a residence. The individual must have owned and occupied the residence as a principal residence for an aggregate of at least two of the five years before the sale.

2. **Income Earned Abroad.** A qualifying individual who works abroad can exclude up to $72,000 of income earned from foreign sources in 1998. The exclusion increases to $80,000 in 2002. To qualify for the exclusion, an American citizen must be a bona fide resident of a foreign country for an entire taxable year or be present in a foreign country for at least 330 days during a 12 consecutive month period.

3. **Exclusions and Other Tax Benefits Related to Higher Education.** Congress has provided a variety of tax benefits to assist taxpayers with higher

education. The Hope Scholarship and Lifetime Learning Credits provide tax credits to low and middle income individuals for tuition expenses. Savings bonds, qualified state tuition programs, and educational IRAs give qualifying individuals tax savings for funding higher education.

4. **Interest on Obligations of States and Local Governments.** Section 103 of the I.R.C. provides that interest on obligations of state and local governments generally is exempt from federal income tax. This tax break allows these governments to borrow money at a reduced rate, since the exclusion of interest will add to the investor's rate of return, particularly an investor in a higher tax bracket. In effect, this is a subsidy from the federal to the state and local governments. The reason behind this exclusion is to encourage investment in state and municipal bonds. Also, it is constitutionally questionable whether taxing these obligations would be an improper infringement on state and local government.

5. **Limitations on Tax-Exempt Interest.** The rules relating to tax-exempt obligations have been limited by the Tax Reform Acts of 1984 and 1986. As a consequence, there are limitations as to the amount and purpose of bond issues that can be tax exempt. Generally, bonds issued for traditional government activities such as roads, schools, etc., will be available without limit. However, "private activity" bonds will be subject to limitations as to specific uses as well as amounts. Beginning in 1988, the amount of "private activity" bonds was limited to the greater of $50 per resident or $150 million per state.

III. IDENTIFICATION OF THE PROPER TAXPAYER

A. INTRODUCTION

Generally, an item of income is taxed to the person who earned it or who owns the producing property. However, the progressive tax rates encourage attempts to divide income among family members or other entities, and in so doing reduce the earner's total tax liability. In the income tax area there are both statutory and judge-made restraints on the "assignment of income," and these provisions may be mandatory or elective.

1. **Mandatory.** An example of a mandatory provision is I.R.C. section 73, which provides that a dependent child's income is taxable to her and not to her parents.

2. **Elective.** Certain income-splitting provisions are available to married couples. Since 1948, married couples have been allowed to split their income as though each spouse had earned one-half of the total. The 1948 law came in response to the inequities that arose from community property states (unlike common law states) allowing married couples to split their income, regardless of who actually earned it.

B. ASSIGNMENT OF INCOME

1. **Income from Services.**

   a. **Anticipatory contracts--**

Lucas v. Earl, 281 U.S. 111 (1930).

Facts. Earl (D) entered into a contract with his wife in which they agreed that any income either of them earned would be owned by them as joint tenants. D claims that due to this contract, he can only be taxed on one-half of his income. The Commissioner (P) and the Board of Tax Appeals held that D should be taxed on the whole of his income. The court of appeals reversed, and P appeals.

Issue. Does a contract allow an earner of income to prevent his salary from vesting for tax purposes?

Held. No. Judgment reversed.

♦ I.R.C. section 61(a) taxes the net income of every individual "derived from salaries, wages, or compensation for personal services." The statute does not seek to tax only income beneficially received, but also that which is actually earned. One cannot by agreement attribute fruits to a different tree from that on which they grew.

---

b. Anticipatory assignments--

Commissioner v. Giannini, 129 F.2d 638 (9th Cir. 1942).

Facts. Giannini (D) was president of Bancitaly Corporation. From 1919 to 1925, he received no compensation. In June 1927, the board of directors approved a plan whereby D would receive 5% of the net profits each year. For the first half of the year, this amounted to $445,704.20. When he found that he would receive this amount, D refused to accept any other compensation for 1927 and suggested that the board do something worthwhile with the money. The board subsequently decided to donate the amount which would have been D's salary for the last half of the year ($1.5 million) to the University of California to establish a Foundation for Agricultural Economics in D's honor. Based on a revised profit estimate, the corporation donated only $1,357,607.40, and D personally donated the difference of $142,392.60. D did not report any part of the $1,357,607.40 as income, and the Commissioner (P) assessed a deficiency, contending that half the amount should have been reported by D and half by his wife. P argued that: (i) actual receipt of money or property is not necessary to constitute taxable income; (ii) it is rather the "realization" of taxable income that gives rise to tax; (iii) the taxpayer "realizes" income when he directs the disposition thereof so that it reaches the object of his bounty; (iv) D had the right to receive the entire 5% as compensation for his services; and (v) waiver of that right and suggestion that the money be applied elsewhere was such a disposition as to amount to liability for income "realized." D argued that: (i) his renunciation of the property legally amounted to an "abandonment" of his rights without a transfer of the rights to another; and (ii) property that is abandoned cannot be "diverted" or "assigned" by the renouncer and thus cannot be taxed upon the theory that it was received. The Board of Tax Appeals held for D, and P appeals.

Issue. When a taxpayer, by anticipatory assignment, makes a gift of the interest or compensation that he is entitled to receive at a future date in return for his present services, does he thereby realize taxable income?

Held. Yes. Judgment affirmed on other grounds.

♦ When a taxpayer makes an anticipatory assignment of compensation that he is to receive at a later date in return for his present services, he nevertheless realizes income. It is as if he had received the compensation and then directly paid it to the donee. The courts have consistently held that income is realized by the assignor who owns or controls the disposition of amounts owed him.

♦ However, this case is different. D neither received the money nor directed its disposition. He made an unqualified refusal to accept the money and only suggested that it be used for some worthwhile purpose. The corporation could have kept the money, and all arrangements for its disposition were handled by the corporation.

♦ There is no evidence that this transaction was a fraud intended to save D and his wife income taxes.

---

c. **Criteria for assignment.** In Revenue Ruling 66-167, a taxpayer elected not to receive compensation for services as executor of his deceased wife's estate. The main consideration was whether the waiver involved would at least primarily constitute evidence of an intent to render a gratuitous service. The taxpayer was determined not to be in receipt of taxable income of the amounts he would otherwise have received as fees and commissions. In Revenue Ruling 74-581, the IRS allowed law school professors to assign their income from legal clinics and services to their law school and successfully shift their income. The following are some of the factors that are considered in determining whether personal services can be assigned: (i) Would the taxpayer normally be expected to receive the income? (ii) What was the relationship between the assigning parties? (iii) Who bore any risk of loss? (iv) Did the assignor of the income receive something in return close to fair market value?

2. **Income from Property.**

a. **Interest coupons--**

Helvering v. Horst, 311 U.S. 112 (1940).

Facts. Horst (D) owned bonds with detachable interest coupons. D delivered the coupons to his son as a gift. When the coupons matured, D's son cashed them. The Commissioner (P) and the Board of Tax Appeals held D taxable for the bond interest. The court of appeals reversed, and P appeals.

Issue. Should the donor be taxed for bond interest when he gave the interest coupons to another before maturity?

Held. Yes. Judgment reversed.

♦ Income is realized by the assignor when he diverts the payment that he could have received to the donee. This satisfies a want of the donor who, in a real sense, enjoys compensation from such fulfillment.

---

b. The *Blair* rule--

Blair v. Commissioner, 300 U.S. 5 (1937).

Facts. Blair (P) was to receive the income from a trust created by his father. P assigned interests in the trust to his children. The trustees accepted the assignments and paid the trust income directly to the assignees. The Commissioner (D) held the assignments to be taxable to P, but the Board of Tax Appeals reversed his decision. The court of appeals reversed, and P appeals.

Issue. Can a beneficiary avoid taxation on trust income by assigning his interests in the trust to others?

Held. Yes. Judgment reversed.

- The one who is to receive the income as the owner of the beneficial interest is to pay the tax. If the interest is assignable without reservation, the assignee thus becomes the beneficiary.

- P's interest in the trust was present property alienable like any other. P could thus transfer a part of his interest as well as the whole. Here, the assignees became the owners of a specified beneficial interest, a form of property (not a chose in action), and the income arising therein is taxable to them.

Comment. It is possible to distinguish *Blair* and *Horst*, *supra*, by analyzing to what extent the donor in each case retained the corpus or the source of the income. In *Horst*, despite a dissenting view that the coupons were independent of the bonds, the bonds were the actual source of the income. In *Blair*, the donor assigned an interest in a trust. The Court stated, "The assignment of the beneficial interest is not the assignment of a chose in action but of the 'right, title, and estate in and to property.'" A portion of the source of the income was given up by the donor in *Blair*. In *Horst*, this corpus was retained by the donor.

---

c. Anticipatory assignment for value--

Estate of Stranahan v. Commissioner, 472 F.2d 867 (6th Cir. 1973).

Facts. In 1964, Stranahan (P) paid the government $754,816 in interest for past tax deficiencies. Since his 1965 income was not large enough to absorb this large interest deduction, P arranged to accelerate his future income. P assigned to his son $122,820 in anticipated future stock dividends. For this, P's son paid P $115,000, which P reported as ordinary income. The Commissioner (D) assessed P with a deficiency, and the Tax Court sided with D, stating that the assignment was in reality a loan masquerading as a sale. P appeals.

Issue. May a shareholder assign his rights to future dividends for value in order to minimize his taxes?

Held. Yes. Judgment reversed.

♦   This transaction was economically realistic, with substance, and should be recognized. A taxpayer is not prohibited from arranging his financial affairs to minimize his taxes. Here, the purchase price was adequate and there were no claims that the transaction was a sham. P's son paid fair consideration to receive future income. The presence of tax avoidance motives will not nullify an otherwise bona fide transaction.

Comment. In most similar cases, the appellate courts have held assignments of future income for immediate consideration to be loans. Had this been the case here, P could not have claimed the dividend income until he actually received the dividends from the corporation.

---

d.   **Conveyance prior to sale--**

Susie Salvatore, 29 T.C.M. 89 (1970).

Facts. Susie Salvatore's husband ran an oil and gas station in Connecticut. When he died, he devised the station to her. For many years their children ran the station, and Susie drew $100 per week for her own support, the balance going to those children working in the business. In 1963, Texaco made an offer of $295,000 for the station and the land. In a family conference, the family agreed to accept the offer and decided that the money would first be used to satisfy an $8,000 tax lien, next to pay a $50,000 mortgage to Texaco, then Susie would receive $100,000, the amount needed to keep up her $100 per week income for life, and the balance would be divided among her children. In July, the agreement to sell was signed, and Texaco made a down payment of $29,500. In August, Susie conveyed one-half interest in the property to her five children by warranty deed recorded September 6, 1963. On August 28 and 30, Susie and the children conveyed their respective interests to Texaco, the deeds being recorded September 6, 1963. Texaco then tendered the remaining $215,582.12. Susie received $118,541 (one-half of the net proceeds). Susie filed a gift tax return reporting gifts to each of her children of one-tenth interest and paid gift tax of $10,744.35. In her income tax return, she reported $115,063 capital gain and an ordinary gain of $665 as her share of the gain from the sale. The children all reported their proportionate shares. The Commissioner determined that Susie's gain on the sale totaled $238,856, all long-term capital gain. The Commissioner argued that Susie's conveyance of the property to her children without consideration was merely an intermediate step in the transfer of legal title to Texaco. Thus, the children were merely "conduits through which to pass title," and the entire sale was attributable to Susie.

Issue. Is a taxpayer liable for the entire gain realized on a sale when she has used other parties as instrumentalities through which to pass title?

Held. Yes. Decision for the Commissioner.

♦ A sale by one person cannot be transformed for tax purposes into a sale by another by using the latter as a conduit through which to pass title. Susie owned the station when she agreed to sell it. Her conveyance to the children, when viewed as a part of the whole transaction, was only an intermediate step in the transfer of legal title to Texaco.

♦ While in form the gift was complete prior to the sale, in substance Susie made an anticipatory assignment of one-half the income of the sale of the property. The artificiality of treating this as a sale in part by her children is shown by the fact that Susie was to receive approximately $5,000 annually, regardless of the sale price of the property.

---

e. **Income from gift.** When a gift is made, if there is a right to collect income on the gift in the future, the donor is taxed on the amount of that right to income that has accrued as of the date of the gift. In Revenue Ruling 69-102, the taxpayer sold a life insurance contract to a charity for an amount equal to his basis therein, and gifted the remaining interest to the charity. He also gave an annuity contract to his son. When the contracts matured the next year, both the charity and the son surrendered them for their cash surrender values. The taxpayer was taxed on the excess of the cash surrender value of each contract at the time of the gift over the taxpayer's basis in the contract even though he had given away the contracts. The taxpayer was held to be in receipt of taxable income in the year in which the contracts were surrendered.

C. INCOME PRODUCING ENTITIES

1. **Trusts.** Trust income is taxed to the grantor who created the trust, the trust itself, or the beneficiary of the trust. Since income from property is normally taxed to its owner, a threshold issue is whether the grantor has sufficient control over the trust to be considered its owner.

    a. **Income taxable to the grantor.** Sections 671 through 678 of the I.R.C. spell out the types of grantor control that impose taxability for trust income on the grantor. Incorporated in this outline are cases that were the forerunners to these I.R.C. sections.

1) Power to revoke or alter the trust--

Corliss v. Bowers, 281 U.S. 376 (1930).

Facts. Corliss (P) transferred an income-raising fund to a trust to pay the income to his wife for life with the remainder to their children. P reserved the power to "modify or alter in any manner, or revoke in whole or in part, this indenture and the trusts then existing." In district court, the Commissioner (D) claimed that the income should be taxable to P. The district court held for D, and the court of appeals affirmed. P appeals.

Issue. Can the grantor be taxed on income that was actually paid to the beneficiary?

Held. Yes. Judgment affirmed.

◆ I.R.C. section 676 provides that "when the grantor of a trust has, at any time during the taxable year, . . . the power to revest in himself title to any part of the corpus of the trust, then the income of such part of the trust . . . shall be included in the net income of the grantor." Income that is subject to a taxpayer's unfettered command and that he is free to enjoy at his own option is taxable to him whether or not he exercises such command.

Comment. Section 676 provides that if the grantor or other nonadverse party (*i.e.,* nonbeneficiary) has the power to revoke the trust after its inception and revest all or part of the corpus in the grantor, he may be taxed for the trust income. Section 674 provides that if the parties above have control over *who* gets the corpus or income or *when* it will be available, the income is taxable to the grantor. However, independent trustees, although nonadverse, may apportion income or corpus among beneficiaries without coming under the section 674 restriction.

---

2) Power to use trust income to discharge grantor's legal obligations--

Morrill v. United States, 288 F. Supp. 734 (S.D. Me. 1964).

Facts. In April 1959, Morrill (P) established four short-term trusts, one for the benefit of each of his four minor children, and named a corporate trustee for each trust. The trust income was to be accumulated and paid to the beneficiary at age 21. The trusts also provided that the trustee had the discretion to use the trust income to pay for the children's educational expenses. After 10 years the trusts were to terminate and the corpus was to revert to P. The children attended five schools during the years in question. In two schools, P expressly assumed responsibility for payment of expenses. The other schools each sent P their bills, which he forwarded, with his check to cover all but room and tuition expenses, to the trustee. The trustee then mailed P's check and a trust-fund check to cover tuition and room to the schools. In filing income tax returns for the years 1959 through 1961, P and his wife did not declare any of the income of the trusts. The Commissioner (D) determined that the amounts used to pay tuition and room were used to satisfy legal obligations of P and were therefore taxable as income to P under I.R.C. section 677. P paid under protest and sues for a refund.

Issue. Is trust income used to satisfy the legal obligation of a grantor income to the grantor?

Held. Yes. Judgment for D.

♦ A long line of cases has interpreted section 677 to mean that trust income that is used to satisfy a legal obligation of the grantor is, in effect, distributed to him and is therefore taxable to him. Treasury Regulation section 1.677(a)-1(d) repeats this fundamental principle.

♦ The income is taxable to the grantor when used to discharge his individual obligation, whether imposed by law or by contract. There is no evidence that the schools looked primarily to the children or only to the trusts for payment. These were expenses that P had assumed either explicitly or by implied contract.

Comment. Section 677 makes the grantor taxable for trust income if he or a nonadverse party has the power to apply the income for the benefit of the grantor or the grantor's spouse. This includes premiums on the grantor's life insurance or aid in supporting the grantor's dependents.

----

3) Other powers--

Helvering v. Clifford, 309 U.S. 331 (1940).

Facts. Clifford (P) put securities in a trust for his wife and designated himself as trustee. The trust was to last for five years, at which time it would revert to P. P as trustee had (among other powers) the power to exercise the voting power of the trust stock, sell or exchange any of the trust stock, invest trust income at his discretion, and compromise his claims as trustee. P did not claim the trust income since he paid gift taxes when he put the stock in trust. The Commissioner (D) assessed P with a deficiency for the trust income. The Board of Tax Appeals upheld the deficiency, but the court of appeals reversed, bringing this appeal from D.

Issue. Does a grantor retain ownership of trust property when he retains unfettered control over it?

Held. Yes. Judgment reversed.

♦ In substance, P's control over the corpus was in all essential respects the same after the trust was created as before. The wide powers that he retained included for all practical purposes most of the control that he as an individual would have. Also, the short duration of the trust and the fact that P's wife is the beneficiary all point to P as the substantive owner of the trust and therefore liable for the trust income.

Dissent (Roberts, McReynolds, JJ.). The Court's decision disregards the fundamental principle that legislation is Congress's function—not the judiciary's.

Comment. Prior to 1987, I.R.C. section 673 taxed the grantor for trust income if he retained a reversionary interest taking effect within 10 years. However, the Tax Reform Act of 1986 eliminated the 10-year reversion rule. The new law provides that a grantor will be taxed on the income of the trust if he has a reversionary interest with a value greater than 5% of the value of the trust.

---

4) **Others treated as trust owners.** If a trust beneficiary has the powers enumerated in this section, she could be taxed for trust income, the same as a grantor.

b. **Income not taxable to the grantor or another person as an owner.** Assuming that the grantor has not retained substantial "strings" or powers over the trust, the trust itself will be recognized as a separate taxable entity. Generally, the income that is distributed to the beneficiaries is taxed to them. The trust only pays tax on the income it retains. The taxable income of a trust is known as *distributable net income* ("DNI"). This is the net income of the trust without deducting distributions to beneficiaries or undistributed capital gains allocated to the trust corpus. Except for these and a few other modifications, the DNI is the trust's net income.

1) **Simple trusts.**

a) **Definition.** A trust that requires all of its income to be distributed to the beneficiaries without adding any of the income to the trust corpus is a simple trust. Also, in a simple trust, no amount of income may be used for charitable purposes. [I.R.C. §651(a)]

b) **Taxation.** In a simple trust, income is taxed to the beneficiaries instead of to the trust. This is done by giving the trust a deduction for all distributions made during the year. The trust's DNI is the maximum amount that the trust may deduct or on which the beneficiaries can be taxed. For example, if trust income (under state law) were $5,600 but DNI were only $5,000, the excess $600 could be distributed tax free.

2) Complex trusts.

    a) Definition. If the trustee has the discretionary power to distribute or accumulate income or to distribute trust corpus, the trust is a complex trust.

    b) Taxation. I.R.C. section 662(a) uses a two-tier approach in taxing complex trusts. Distributions are classified into the first or second tier.

        (1) First tier. Income that is required to be currently distributed is a first-tier distribution.

        (2) Second tier. Discretionary amounts that the trustee allows to be paid to certain beneficiaries are second-tier distributions.

        (3) Example. DNI is allocated to the first-tier distributions, with the remainder prorated among the second tier. Suppose that DNI is $13,000 and the trust instrument requires $10,000 to be paid to A. The trustee decides to make discretionary payments of $4,000 to B and $2,000 to C. A's entire distribution is taxable under the first tier. This leaves only $3,000 available for the second tier, which is prorated between B and C. B is taxed on $2,000 and A on $1,000.

3) Unlimited throwback rule. A low-tax-bracket trust used to be a good tax-saving device. A high-bracket taxpayer would allow trust income to accumulate in the trust, and the trust could be taxed on it at lower rates. Then, in subsequent years, the taxpayer could receive the income tax free to the extent that it exceeded the subsequent year's DNI. The throwback rules (I.R.C. sections 665 through 668) take away this tax-saving device. Those rules provide that when a trust accumulates distribution income, the income will be taxed to the beneficiaries as if it had been received by them in the earliest tax year in which the trust had undistributed net income.

c. Multiple trusts. I.R.C. section 643(e) provides that multiple trusts that incorporate the same grantor and beneficiary and have as their principal motive tax avoidance must be consolidated and treated as one trust. This, along with the throwback rules, mitigates any tax advantage of multiple trusts.

d. **Income in respect of decedents.** I.R.C. section 691 addresses the problem of income earned but not yet recognized at the date of a person's death. In general, income is included in the gross income of the estate, or in the other person who receives the right to such income as a result of the death of the decedent. The income is recognized in the year in which it is received.

2. **Partnerships.**

a. **Taxation of partnerships in general.** Sections 701 through 761 (subchapter K) of the I.R.C. cover partnerships. Partnerships are not subject to income tax, but are required to file tax returns showing net income or loss. The individual partners are subject to income tax on their shares of the partnership income. For this reason, the partnership is considered to be a "conduit" through which the partnership income or loss flows through to the individual partners. The individual partner, however, does not merely claim the single net figure on her tax return. The separate characterizations of income and loss retain their nature as they are taken by each partner. Thus, one partner could claim a long-term capital gain as well as an ordinary operating loss from the same partnership. The characterization of an item of income or deduction is determined at the partnership level, without regard to the individual partners who ultimately claim the item.

b. **Family partnerships--**

Commissioner v. Culbertson, 337 U.S. 733 (1949).

Facts. Culbertson (P) operated a cattle business partnership with Coon. Coon agreed to sell his interest to P if P would sell a one-half interest to P's sons because Coon wanted the business to continue but felt P was too old to carry on alone. P's sons paid for their interest through gifts and loans from P. During the tax year, three of the sons worked on the ranch (two only during the summer, however) while a fourth was in the army. The Commissioner (D) disallowed P's attempt to split the partnership income with his sons. The Tax Court sustained the Commissioner, but the court of appeals reversed.

Issue. May family members split income when forming a partnership?

Held. Yes. Case remanded.

♦ In determining whether a family partnership will be recognized for tax purposes, two considerations must be met. The Tax Court stated that to become a bona fide member of a family partnership, a partner must contribute either "vital services" or "original capital." This test is not sufficient. Most important is a showing by the partners that they acted in good faith and with a business purpose in entering into the family partnership. A business purpose must be something more than tax avoidance.

---

c. ***Culbertson* requirements relaxed.** Congress has substantially relaxed the requirements of *Culbertson*. Where capital is a "material income-producing fact" in the partnership, the gift will effectively shift income, even if the donee contributes neither capital nor services. [I.R.C. §702(e)]

    1) **Reasonable compensation.** The Commissioner can require that the donor receive reasonable compensation for her services before anything is left to be divided with the children. This is to insure that personal service income is taxed to the one doing the work; supposedly only the return from capital can be divided with the children.

    2) **Sham transfers.** The Commissioner frequently argues that there has been ***no real transfer*** of partnership interests to the children and thus that the transfer is a sham. Treasury Regulation section 1.704-1(e) states that the controlling factor is whether the contributor of the capital is the actual owner of the capital.

    3) **Materiality of capital.** If capital is not a "material income-producing factor," the statute does not apply, and the taxpayer must resort to the standards of *Culbertson*.

3. **Corporations.** Unlike partnerships, corporations are assessed an income tax. Currently, the corporate tax brackets are as follows:

Taxable Income	Rate
0 to $50,000	15%
$50,000 to $75,000	25%
$75,000 to $100,000	34%
$100,000 to $335,000	39%
$335,000 to $10,000,000	34%
$10,000,000 to $15,000,000	35%
$15,000,000 to $18,333,333	38%
$18,333,333 and above	35%

a. **Double taxation.** Corporations are taxed on their earnings. When those earnings are distributed to the shareholders as dividends, the shareholders are taxed again on the same earnings. The effect is that corporate earnings are subject to ***double*** taxation. Many cases in this area result from shareholders of closely held corporations taking advantage of the lower corporate tax rates and then trying to get money out of the corporation without the money being taxed as dividends.

b.   Income splitting by stock transfer--

Overton v. Commissioner, 162 F.2d 155 (2d Cir. 1947).

Facts. Overton and Oliphant (Ps) were controlling stockholders of Castle & Overton, Inc. In 1936, they created a new class of corporate stock, which they distributed as a gift on a pro rata basis to their wives. The tax consequence was, of course, to split the income of the husbands. The wives' stock carried no voting rights and only nominal liquidation value. The dividend rights on the wives' stock were calculated to produce income to the wives only after exceeding a certain income level for their husbands. The Commissioner (D) found deficiencies in Overton's gift tax and Oliphant's income tax. This appeal followed.

Issue. May controlling stockholders of a corporation reduce their taxable income by creating stock and transferring it to family members?

Held. No. Orders affirmed.

♦   Transfers of stock that serve no purpose other than to effect an anticipatory assignment of dividend income for tax avoidance purposes are void for such purposes. This conclusion is inescapable unless form is to be exalted over substance. If the husbands had been content to transfer the original stock with its capital value, voting rights, and liquidation rights, the transfer could have been successful. As it was, however, the transfer was a sham.

c.   Control of earnings--

Johnson v. Commissioner, 78 T.C. 882 (1982).

Facts. Taxpayer (P) was a professional basketball player. He entered into a contract with PMSA granting PMSA the right to his services in exchange for a monthly salary. PMSA assigned its rights to EST, and EST made the payments to P, also remitting 95% of its net revenue to PMSA. P signed a contract to play basketball for the Warriors, and he assigned all of his rights to EST. The Warriors paid their compensation directly to EST.

Issue. Were amounts paid by the Warriors taxable income to P?

Held. Yes.

- In determining that a corporation has earned certain income as opposed to the individual performing the services, two elements must be present. First, the person performing the services must be "an employee of the corporation whom the corporation has the right to direct or control in some meaningful sense." Second, "there must exist between the corporation and the person or entity using the services a contract or similar indicium recognizing the corporation's controlling position."

- In the present case, the contract for services was made directly between P and the Warriors. A contract was not made between the Warriors and PMSA or EST. Since the employment arrangement was between the Warriors and P, the compensation belongs to P and is taxable to P.

---

d. **Reallocation of income between entities--**

Borge v. Commissioner, 405 F.2d 673 (2d Cir. 1968), *cert. denied*, 395 U.S. 933 (1969).

Facts. Victor Borge (P) operated a poultry company from 1952 to 1958. He deducted the substantial losses sustained by the company from his personal income as a prominent entertainer. Subsequently, he formed a corporation, Danica, and transferred the poultry business to the corporation in return for all of its stock. P made an agreement with Danica to perform entertainment and promotional services for the corporation in return for a salary of $50,000 per year. Danica was then able to offset the poultry losses against the much larger entertainment profits. It was shown that Danica did nothing to aid P in his entertainment business. In fact, the $50,000 salary was paid only in 1962. Under I.R.C. section 482, the Commissioner (D) reallocated to P from Danica $75,000 per year from 1958 to 1961, and $25,000 for 1962. D found that for purposes of section 482, P owned or controlled the two businesses—an entertainment business and a poultry business—but that he had merely assigned the income from the entertainment business to Danica, which had done nothing to earn that income. D was sustained by the Tax Court. P appeals, arguing that P as an individual was not an "organization, trade, or business."

Issue. Can D utilize section 482 to reallocate income between two organizations, trades, or businesses that are controlled or owned by the same parties to more clearly reflect a taxpayer's true income or prevent tax evasion?

Held. Yes. Judgment affirmed.

- Under the general provision of section 482, D was not mistaken in determining that P was operating a "business" as an entertainer.

♦   Under section 482, the Commissioner may redistribute or apportion the income, deductions, etc., between or among two or more organizations, trades, or businesses that are owned or controlled by the same interests, if he deems such apportionment necessary to clearly reflect income or to prevent evasion of tax. P was channeling a part of his income as an entertainer through a corporation that did nothing to help earn the income. The sole purpose was to permit Danica to offset losses, and thus D's reallocation was necessary to accurately reflect the income of the two businesses under P's common control.

Comment. Whenever the lack of an arm's length relationship produces a different economic result than would occur in the case of two uncontrolled parties dealing at arm's length, the Commissioner is authorized to allocate gross income and deductions.

IV. DEDUCTIONS IN COMPUTING TAXABLE INCOME

A. INTRODUCTION

Deductions, unlike gross income, are recognized for tax purposes as a matter of "legislative grace." In order to claim a deduction, taxpayers must find a specific code section that specifically allows the deduction. Two motivations dictate the federal income tax use of deductions and credits: (i) to tax only net income, and (ii) to encourage certain activities or investments. The various deductions are detailed in sections 151 through 250 of the I.R.C. Certain nondeductible items are mentioned in sections 261 through 280G of the I.R.C.

B. BUSINESS EXPENSES

1. **Introduction.** Section 162 of the I.R.C. provides that "all the ordinary and necessary expenses paid or incurred during the taxable year in carrying on a trade or business" are deductible. Three issues frequently arise in this context: (i) Was the expense "ordinary and necessary"? (ii) Was the expenditure a current expense or a capital outlay? and (iii) Was the expense for business or personal reasons? The deductible business expense is the most important single deduction in the I.R.C.

2. **"Ordinary and Necessary" Expenses--**

Welch v. Helvering, 290 U.S. 111 (1933).

Facts. Welch (P) was the secretary of a grain company that was adjudged bankrupt and discharged from its debts. To aid in his relations with customers and to solidify his own credit standing, P paid some of the debts of his former employer. The Commissioner ruled that these were not ordinary and necessary business expenses, but were rather in the nature of capital outlays for development of goodwill. The Board of Tax Appeals and the court of appeals both affirmed, and P appeals.

Issue. Are payments by a taxpayer to the creditors of his bankrupt former employer deductible if they were made to strengthen his own credit position and personal reputation?

Held. No. Judgment affirmed.

◆   Ordinary and necessary business expenses are defined according to the normal means of conduct and forms of speech in the business world. Paying another's debts does not fall within this definition.

♦   By the usage of trade, paying debts without legal obligation is extraordinary, even if done for the purpose of strengthening one's own credit. This is not the normal method of dealing with this type of business situation (*i.e.,* it is not an ordinary expense of doing business).

Comment. A taxpayer's payment of another's expenses or debts is not deductible unless the purpose of making the payment is to directly further or promote his own business.

---

3.   Deductible Expense or Capital Expenditure--

Midland Empire Packing Co. v. Commissioner, 14 T.C. 635 (1950).

Facts. Midland (P) had been using the basement of its plant for curing meat and storing hides for 25 years when it discovered that oil was seeping into the area. P installed a concrete lining on the floor and walls to solve the problem and deducted the oilproofing costs as an ordinary business expense. The Commissioner (D) disallowed the deduction, claiming it to be a capital improvement adding to the depreciable basis of the building.

Issue. Should a building improvement that does not add to the useful life or value of the building be capitalized?

Held. No. D's decision is overturned.

♦   When expenditure adds nothing of value to an asset but merely maintains it, it is an ordinary and necessary business expense. The oilproofing kept the property in operating condition but did not add to its life.

Comment. Section 263(a)(1) provides that deductions may not be taken for amounts "paid out for new buildings or for permanent improvements or betterments made to increase the value of any property." Some of the criteria distinguishing capitalizations from expenses are:

(i)   Whether the expenditure prolongs the life of the property;

(ii)   Whether the improvements will endure over and beyond the taxable year;

(iii)   Whether the expenditure adds to the value of the property;

(iv)   Whether the expenditure was part of an overall improvement or only a replacement of minor or recurring items; and

(v)   Whether there is a change or alteration in use or function.

4. Expenditure for Future Benefit--

Indopco, Inc. v. Commissioner, 503 U.S. 79 (1992)

Facts. Indopco, Inc. (P) manufactures adhesives, starches, and specialty chemical products. In October 1977, Unilever United States, Inc. expressed interest in acquiring P through a friendly transaction. In November 1977, a formal acquisition transaction was proposed to P's directors. To ensure that the transaction would be fair to P's stockholders, P incurred significant consulting fees in the process of evaluating the transaction and in obtaining a fairness opinion. On P's federal tax return for the short year ending August 15, 1978, P claimed a deduction for $2,225,586 paid to its investment banker but did no deduct $505,069 paid to P's legal counsel. Upon audit, the Commissioner (D) disallowed the deduction. P sought redetermination in the Tax Court, claiming that both the banking fees and legal fees should be currently deductible since these expenditures did not create or enhance a separate and distinct additional asset. The Third Circuit Court of Appeals affirmed the Tax Court's decision that the expenditures must be capitalized since P received long-term benefits from the Unilever acquisition.

Issue. Can expenditures that benefit a taxpayer for an indefinite period into the future, but do not create or enhance a separate and distinct asset, be deducted currently as "ordinary and necessary" business expenses under IRC section 162(a)?

Held. No. Judgment of court of appeals affirmed.

♦ Expenses incurred for the purpose of changing corporate structure for the benefit of future operations are not ordinary and necessary expenses.

Comment. The IRS has issued several rulings subsequent to the *Indopco* decision regarding various types of expenditures that may provide long-term benefits. One can expect capitalization controversies to continue as the Commissioner and taxpayers try to apply *Indopco* to different situations.

5. "Carrying On" Business--

Morton Frank v. Commissioner, 20 T.C. 511 (1953).

Facts. Morton Frank and his wife spent about one year traveling around the country in an attempt to locate a newspaper or radio station to buy and operate. They deducted their travel and other related expenses. The Commissioner determined a deficiency, and Frank appeals to the Tax Court.

Issue. Under I.R.C. section 162(a), may travel expenses in searching for a business to purchase and operate be deducted as an ordinary and necessary business expense?

Held. No. Judgment for the Commissioner.

♦ Deductible expenses may be incurred only in connection with the operation of an *existing* business. The Franks were not engaged in a business when the expenses were incurred; the trips were preparatory to entering into a business. Thus, the expenses are not deductible.

Comment. I.R.C. section 195 allows taxpayers to amortize "start-up" costs over five years. Start-up costs are defined as amounts incurred in investigation, creation, or acquisition of an active trade or business. However, such costs are limited to those that would otherwise be deductible if the taxpayer was already engaged in such trade or business.

C. SPECIFIC BUSINESS DEDUCTIONS

1. "Reasonable" Salaries.

a. Seven factor test--

Exacto Spring Corporation v. Commissioner, 196 F.3d 833 (7th Cir. 1999).

Facts. Exacto Spring Corporation (P) paid its co-founder, chief executive, and principal owner, William Heitz, $1.3 million in 1993 and $1.0 million in 1994 in salary. The IRS (D) claimed that these amounts were excessive and reduced the salary deduction to $381,000 in 1993 and $400,000 in 1994. In evaluating the case the Tax Court applied a test that uses seven factors, none entitled to any specified weight relative to another, to determine if the salary was reasonable. The factors are: (i) the type and extent of services rendered; (ii) the scarcity of qualified employees; (iii) the qualifications and prior earning capacity of the employee; (iv) the contributions of the employee to the business; (v) the net earnings of the employer; (vi) the prevailing compensation paid to employees with comparable jobs; and (vii) the peculiar characteristics of the employer's business. The Tax Court split the difference between D and P roughly in half by allowing compensation of $900,000 in 1993 and $700,000 in 1994. P appeals.

Issue. Was the original salary paid to Heitz reasonable?

Held. Yes. Judgment reversed.

♦ Based on the facts and circumstances, all of the seven factors either favor the taxpayer or are neutral. It is unclear how the Tax Court arrived at its decision to limit P's compensation. Based upon the "independent investor" test, the compensation was reasonable.

Comment. The Seventh Circuit became the first to abandon the multi-factor approach in favor of the "independent investor" test. Under this test, compensation is considered reasonable when the employer's unrelated investors are still earning a reasonable return on their investment. Courts considering reasonable compensation after this case have still used the seven-factor test, while sometimes supplementing it with the independent investor test.

---

b. Percentage salary as valid business expense--

Harolds Club v. Commissioner, 340 F.2d 861 (9th Cir. 1965).

Facts. Smith had engaged in several gaming operations prior to 1935, when he decided to open a club in Nevada called "Harolds" (P). Smith's 25-year-old son, Harold, was designated as the owner of the club. Later, another son, Raymond, was made a partner with Harold. The club was a success under Smith's management. In 1941, it was decided to pay Smith a salary of $10,000 per year, plus 20% of the club's profits. Smith's salaries from 1952 to 1956 ranged from $350,201 to $557,560. P deducted these salaries as a business expense. The Commissioner found that the salary was unreasonable, and the Tax Court found that the portion above 15% of the profits was unreasonable and thus not deductible for tax purposes as an ordinary business expense. P appeals.

Issue. Was Smith's salary reasonable and therefore a valid business expense for tax purposes?

Held. No, not to the extent of the amounts above 15% of the club's profits. Judgment affirmed.

♦ Contingent compensation is ordinarily allowed as a deduction even though it may be greater than the amount ordinarily paid, if paid pursuant to a "free bargain" between the employer and the individual. Here the agreement was not the result of a free bargain, due to Smith's position and dominance as the father of the owners of the club (*i.e.,* Harold and Raymond acquiesced in virtually all of Smith's decisions).

Comment. A salary based on a percentage of income or profits is deductible even if unreasonable (in terms of the work performed versus the amount of compensation received) if it is found that a "free bargain" was entered into in setting the compensation amount.

---

c. **Shareholder-employees.** Corporations frequently attempt to deduct as business expenses large salaries paid to executives who are also shareholders of the corporation. The IRS tries to get these salaries classified as nondeductible dividends. Salary payments that have no real relationship to the value of the services rendered are therefore not deductible as ordinary business expenses.

d. **"Golden parachute" payments.** I.R.C. section 280G restricts deductions for substantial bonuses paid to corporate executives contingent on the change in control of the company. The amount disallowed is based on a formula that factors in the taxpayer's average compensation for a five-year period.

2. **Travel "Away from Home."** I.R.C. section 162(a)(2) allows the deduction of expenses for traveling, meals, and lodging while "away from home" and "in the pursuit of a trade or business."

a. **"Away from home."**

1) **Definition--**

Rosenspan v. United States, 438 F.2d 905 (2d Cir. 1971), *cert. denied*, 404 U.S. 864 (1971).

Facts. Rosenspan (P) was a traveling jewelry salesman. He was on the road almost all the time and did not maintain a home anywhere, although he received mail and registered for voting purposes at his brother's home in Brooklyn. His employers' headquarters were in New York. Under I.R.C. section 162, which allows deductions for meals and lodging "while away from home in the pursuit of a trade or business," P deducted the meal and lodging expenses incurred on his trips. The Commissioner (D) disallowed the deduction, arguing that Rosenspan did not fit under the provision because he had no "home" to be "away from." The district court dismissed P's action for a refund, and P appeals.

Issue. Does I.R.C. section 162 allow a deduction for travel expenses while away from home for a traveling salesman who does not maintain a permanent home?

Held. No. Judgment affirmed.

♦ Three conditions must be satisfied to receive the deduction: (i) the expense must be reasonable and necessary; (ii) the expense must be incurred in pursuit of a business; and (iii) the expense must be incurred "while away from home." P satisfies the first two conditions, but not the third. He has no home to be away from.

♦ Although in the past D has defined "home" as "business headquarters," courts have rejected this position and the Supreme Court has declined to rule on the issue. Food and lodging are normally personal (nondeductible) expenses. The original intent of this provision was to allow as a deduction the *excess* over "home" food and lodging expenses caused by business travel. However, because of the extreme difficulty in calculating the excess, Congress allowed the entire expense while away from home. To allow this type of deduction if a taxpayer has no home would frustrate the underlying rationale of the provision.

---

2) Taxpayers with multiple "homes"--

Andrews v. Commissioner, 931 F.2d 132 (1st Cir. 1991).

Facts. Edward Andrews (P) operated a swimming pool construction company in New England. P also owned two racehorse breeding farms in Florida. P spent most of the summer months working in Massachusetts in the pool construction business and resided in Florida in the winter months, training horses and running the horse operations. P began to spend so much time in Florida that he eventually bought a condominium in Florida and later replaced the condominium with a single family home. In 1984, P worked in Florida for six months, from January through April and during November and December, and worked in Massachusetts for six months, from May to October. On his 1984 tax return, P deducted his Florida housing and meal costs as travel expenses incurred away from home. The Commissioner (D) disallowed the deduction on the ground that P was not "away from home." The Tax Court sustained D's disallowance of the deduction, and P appeals.

Issue. May a taxpayer claim as a deduction his duplicative living expenses caused by having two businesses that require him to spend a substantial amount of time in each of two widely separate places?

Held. Yes. Judgment vacated and case remanded.

♦ Section 162(a)(2) allows deduction of "traveling expenses . . . while away from home in the pursuit of a trade or business." The purpose of this deduction is to mitigate the burden on a taxpayer who, because of the exigencies of his trade or business, must maintain two places of abode and thereby incur additional living expenses. A taxpayer's home, for purposes of section 162, is the area or vicinity of his principal place of business.

♦ The Tax Court incorrectly held that P had two tax homes. "Where business necessity requires that a taxpayer maintain two places of abode, and thereby incur additional and duplicate living expenses, such duplicate expenses are a cost of producing income and should ordinarily be deductible." The costs associated with maintaining the principal residence are not deductible, but living expenses incurred while on business at the other house are deductible as "away from home" business expenses.

Comment. If the taxpayer is engaged in business at two or more separate locations, the "tax home" for purposes of this deduction is located at the ***principal place of business***

during the taxable year. Travel between the different locations is deductible, but meals and lodging are deductible only when the taxpayer is at a location that is not "home" (*i.e.,* not the principal location).

---

3) **The "sleep or rest" rule.** A taxpayer "away from home" on business may deduct the cost of his meals only if the trip requires him to stop for "sleep or rest."

4) **"Temporary" rule.** The taxpayer is entitled to deduct his transportation, food, and lodging if a job assignment at a distant location is temporary. Revenue Ruling 99-7, 1999-1 C.B. 361, outlines the rules regarding whether a work location is temporary. If at the beginning of the employment, the employment at the work location is realistically expected to last (and does in fact last) for one year or less, the employment is temporary. If the employment was inititially expected to last for one year or less, but later is realistically expected to continue beyond one year, it will be treated as temporary until the taxpayer's realistic expectations change, and then it will be treated as not temporary. If the employment is realistically expected to last for more than one year, it is not temporary, even if it actually lasts one year or less.

b. **"Pursuit of a trade or business."** The expenses must have been incurred primarily in furtherance of business rather than personal objectives.

1) **Commuting expenses.** Expenses incurred in traveling between the taxpayer's residence and his place of work are not deductible as business expenses.

a) Note, however, that travel between business locations *is* deductible.

b) Even if the taxpayer carries work-related materials (*e.g.,* tools) with him, only those extra costs incurred to transport those materials (*e.g.,* trailer rental) are deductible.

2) **Business and pleasure trips.** When a trip is incurred for these dual reasons, the expenses are deductible if the ***primary purpose*** of the trip was business. However, the expenses must be allocated between business and pleasure.

3. **Necessary Rental and Similar Payments.** I.R.C. section 162(a)(3) provides that rental payments for the use of property belonging to another are a deductible business expense.

a. Sale or lease?--

Starr's Estate v. Commissioner, 274 F.2d 294 (9th Cir. 1959).

Facts. Starr (P) had a fire sprinkler system installed in his business. By the terms of the contract, P had a five-year lease of the system for $1,240 per year and an option to renew for an additional five years at $32 per year. P deducted $6,200 as rental expense. The Tax Court sustained the Commissioner's (D's) position that the $6,200 paid was a capital expenditure and not deductible as rental. A depreciation expense of $270 per year was allowed. P appeals.

Issue. Is a lease that provides for a renewal of the lease with nominal payments equivalent to a sale for tax purposes?

Held. Yes. Judgment affirmed in part and reversed in part.

- ◆ To distinguish a lease from a sale, form can be disregarded in favor of substance. In this case, the sprinkler system was tailor-made for P's building, and it seems highly unlikely that it would be repossessed for its negligible salvage value.

- ◆ It is obvious that nominal rental payments of $32 after the lease renewal were nothing more than a service charge. It should be noted that the sprinkler company had never reclaimed a system at the end of the lease term. This transaction was a sale.

Comment. Revenue Ruling 75-21 sets forth guidelines for determining whether a transaction purported to be a lease will be treated as a lease for income tax purposes. A true lease will have the following characteristics:

(i) The lessor will maintain an investment in the property throughout the life of the lease of at least 20% of the property's cost.

(ii) Any lease renewals must be at fair market value at the time of the renewal option.

(iii) The lessee may not have a contractual right to purchase the property at below fair market value.

(iv) A lessee may not furnish part of the leased property's cost or improvements to be retained by the lessor.

(v) No lessee may loan the lessor funds to purchase lease property.

(vi) The lessor must show that there is a reasonable expectation of profit from the lease.

4. **Expenses for Education.**

    a. **General rule.** Educational costs that either qualify the taxpayer for a new trade or business, or that constitute the minimum educational requirement for qualification in her job, are never deductible.

    b. **Deductible educational costs.** As long as they do not fall under the general rule above, the following expenses can be deducted.

        1) **Required for job.** Educational expenses that meet the express requirements of the individual's employer or the requirements of law, as a condition to retention of a job or an increase in the rate of compensation, may be deducted.

            a) **Courses required to renew teaching certificate--**

Hill v. Commissioner, 181 F.2d 906 (4th Cir. 1950).

Facts. Hill (P), a school teacher in Virginia, was required periodically to renew her certificate by either attending summer school courses or passing an exam on selected books. She chose to attend summer school courses at Columbia University, and deducted her expenses on her income tax return. The Commissioner (D) disallowed the deductions on the grounds that they were personal and not business expenses, maintaining that they were neither "ordinary and necessary" nor incurred in carrying on a trade or business. The Tax Court agreed with D that attendance at summer school was not the "ordinary" way to renew the certificate and that there was no evidence that P was employed to continue teaching when she took the courses.

Issue. Are educational expenses required of a teacher to renew her certificate deductible as expenses incurred in carrying on a trade or business?

Held. Yes. Judgment reversed.

♦   Educational expenses incurred by the taxpayer in order to be able to continue to carry on her trade or business are deductible as business expenses. The taxpayer need only show that taking classes is what a reasonable person would do under the specific circumstances. It need not be the only means available to continue in business.

♦   P had been teaching for many years and clearly intended to continue to do so. To say that the education qualified her for reemployment (*i.e.,* a new position) rather than maintaining an employed status is unreal and hypercritical.

2) Improves job skills. Education that *maintains or improves* skills required by the individual in her job or other trade or business is deductible.

a) Courses to remain current in the field--

Coughlin v. Commissioner, 203 F.2d 307 (2d Cir. 1953).

Facts. Coughlin (P) was a tax specialist for his law firm. In 1946, he attended a seminar on federal taxation, held at a New York university, for practicing professionals. He deducted the tuition fee and expenses as ordinary and necessary business expenses. The Commissioner (D) disallowed the deduction, and the Tax Court ruled that the expenses were personal in nature. P appeals.

Issue. Are educational expenses incurred to enhance one's skills required in one's trade or business deductible as business expenses?

Held. Yes. Judgment reversed and case remanded.

♦ Educational expenses incurred to enhance the skills required in the practice of one's trade or business are properly deductible as ordinary and necessary expenses incurred in carrying on a trade or business if "directly connected with" or "proximately resulting from" the practice of that profession.

♦ Tax regulations that prohibit deduction of educational expenses as nonbusiness expenses do not apply to deductions claimed as a business expense. *Hill, supra,* allowed educational expenses that were *required* to carry on a trade or business. The same rule should apply where the practitioner has a moral and professional duty to remain current in the developments in his field. In this case, that duty overshadows any personal benefit gained from the seminar.

---

5. **Miscellaneous Business Deductions.** All ordinary and necessary business expenses are deductible. Those discussed above are the ones specifically listed in section 162(a), but it is impossible to compose an exhaustive list. Those mentioned below are some of the more important business expense deductions. However, starting in 1987, these expenses, when combined with other miscellaneous itemized deductions, became deductible only if they exceed 2% of the taxpayer's adjusted gross income.

   a. **Entertainment.**

      1) **Business meals and entertainment.** The deductions for business meals and entertainment are limited to 80% of such expenses. In

addition, the meal or entertainment must be directly related to the conduct of the taxpayer's active trade or business. There are additional restrictions for meal deductions; in order to deduct 80% of the cost of a meal, the taxpayer or his employee must be present at the meal and the meal must not be lavish.

    2)   **Entertainment facilities.** Membership dues paid for entertainment facilities are deductible if the taxpayer can show that the primary use of the facility was for ordinary and necessary business purposes, and the deduction is limited to this business use.

    3)   **Recordkeeping.** I.R.C. section 274(d) requires that the taxpayer keep adequate records or corroborative evidence supporting his entertainment expense claims. These are scrutinized carefully by the IRS and the courts.

b.   **Summer homes.** I.R.C. section 280A allows limited deductions for homes that are rented out part-time. If a dwelling is used as a personal home for over 14 days or 10% of the days it was rented, it is subject to this section, and expenses must be prorated between rental time and personal time (which is not deductible). Section 280A discusses various other limitations not covered here.

c.   **Uniforms.** Expenses of acquiring and maintaining uniforms used for work are deductible as ordinary and necessary business expenses if (i) the uniform is specifically required as a condition of employment, and (ii) the uniform is not adaptable to continued usage in the place of regular clothing.

d.   **Advertising.** Generally, advertising expenses of a business are deductible in the year incurred even though the effect may last for several years.

    1)   **Signs.** A billboard or sign that will last several years is a capital asset and must be depreciated over several years.

    2)   **Political contributions.** No direct or indirect political contributions can be deducted except by individuals. Thus, advertising in programs for political conventions, etc., is not deductible.

e.   **Dues.** Dues paid to organizations related directly to one's business, such as bar association dues or union dues, are deductible.

f.   **Child-care expenses.** Deducting the costs of child care was traditionally not permitted as a business expense. However, Congress has provided a tax credit for these costs. A taxpayer can claim a credit for up to 35% of the costs of caring for a dependent under age 13 and the costs of household services, if the costs are incurred so that the taxpayer can be employed. The credit cannot exceed $3,000 for one individual and $6,000 for two or more individuals. Also, the expense cannot exceed the earned income of the lower earning spouse (unless a student).

g. **Expenses for tax advice.** I.R.C. section 212(3) allows a deduction for expenses in determining, collecting, or refunding taxes. This covers return preparation, tax litigation, and tax planning expenses.

h. **Business losses.** I.R.C. section 165(c)(1) permits an individual to deduct any loss "incurred in a trade or business."

1) **Realization requirement.** The loss must be "realized," *i.e.,* evidenced by a closed and completed transaction, or fixed by an identifiable event. Mere decline in the value of property is not enough. However, not every closed transaction that results in financial disadvantage qualifies as a loss. For example, a deduction is allowed for loss sustained on demolition of a building used in trade or business or held for rent production. However, if the building was purchased with demolition in mind, the cost of the building would be treated as part of the land cost, and no loss would be allowed.

2) **Amount of deduction.** The amount of loss deductible is the difference between the value of the property immediately preceding the loss and the value of the property immediately afterwards. The difference in value claimed as a loss cannot exceed the adjusted basis of the property and is reduced by any insurance or other compensation received as a result of the loss.

6. **Depreciation.** I.R.C. section 167 permits as a depreciation deduction (*i.e.,* a tax write-off or deduction of part of the basis or cost of a capital asset of limited useful life that is used over a time in producing income) a "reasonable allowance for the exhaustion, wear, and tear" of assets (i) used in a trade or business or (ii) held for the production of income. All physical property used in a trade or business or for the production of income may be depreciated if it has a limited useful life. Also, intangible assets (*e.g.,* copyright) may be depreciated unless their useful life is indefinite. For computing depreciation, first determine whether the property was placed in service before 1981, after 1980 but before 1987, or after 1987. For assets purchased before 1981, the following computations apply. If placed in service after this date but before 1987, the old Accelerated Cost Recovery System ("old ACRS") applies. If placed in service after 1986, the current ACRS applies. These rules are discussed *infra.*

a. **Non-ACRS computation.** Depreciation is computed by taking the cost of the asset (less salvage value) and allocating it over the useful life of the asset by an accepted depreciation method.

1) **Useful life.** The asset depreciation range ("ADR") system [I.R.C. §167(m)] is a list of broad classes of assets with estimated useful lives, published by the IRS. A taxpayer may elect a useful life within 20% of these guidelines, and the IRS will not challenge it. If the taxpayer chooses a useful life outside this range, she has the burden of showing the reasonableness of her estimation.

2) **Methods.** Any "reasonable" method for allocating the cost of the wasting asset over its useful life is acceptable, but may not result in a faster write-off than that allowed by the "double-declining-balance method." I.R.C. section 167 outlines the numerous limitations and rules with respect to depreciation methods, with particular attention given to the rules governing the different declining balance methods. The most common depreciation methods are discussed below.

   a) **Straight-line method.** To compute yearly depreciation, the cost of the property, less salvage value, is divided by the useful life of the property. Suppose that a taxpayer purchases a machine for $10,500 that has a useful life of five years and a salvage value of $500. Each year she could claim depreciation of $2,000 (($10,500 -$500)/5).

   b) **Declining-balance method.** Each year's depreciation is computed by subtracting from the property's basis the amount already written off, and applying a constant rate to the remaining basis. The rate should not be more than twice the rate used in the straight-line method above, and the salvage value is not deducted, but is equal to what remains at the end of the useful life. For example, if a taxpayer purchases a machine for $10,500 with a useful life of five years, she would compute depreciation under the double declining balance method (200% of the straight-line rate) as follows:

Year	Rate	Year's Depreciation	Remaining Basis
			$10,500
1	200%	$4,200	6,300
2	200%	2,520	3,780
3	200%	1,512	2,268
4	200%	907	1,361
5	remainder	544	817
			(salvage)

   c) **Sum-of-the-years-digits method.** Under this method, depreciation is computed by using a changing fraction. The numerator is the remaining years of useful life, and the denominator is the sum of the numbers representing the total of the numerators. For example, the machine in a) above would be depreciated as follows:

Year	Fraction	x	Basis	= Year's Depreciation
1	5/15		$10,000	$3,333
2	4/15		10,000	2,667
3	3/15		10,000	2,000
4	2/15		10,000	1,333
5	1/15		10,000	667

b. **Depreciation in the year of sale.** When property is sold (or purchased) during the taxable year, the taxpayer may claim a pro rata portion of depreciation corresponding with the time of ownership of the asset during that year.

c. **ACRS.** Old ACRS rules in I.R.C. section 168 apply to all tangible depreciable property used in a trade or business or held for the production of income and placed in service after 1980 and before 1987. Current ACRS rules apply to assets placed in service after 1986.

1) **Shorter lives for personal property.** Instead of a system that is based on complicated guideline lives (with permissible shortening up to 20% under the asset depreciation range system), the old ACRS provided for shorter lives for assets placed in service after 1980. The current lives are typically longer than the old ACRS lives. ACRS provides an option for taxpayers who wish to depreciate assets over a slower method and/or over a longer life.

a) **Limitation.** Under both the old and current ACRS, limits are placed on the deductions for cars and home computers used for business. Unless the business use of any car or home computer is more than 50% of its total use, only straight line (not ACRS) depreciation can be used.

d. **Current ACRS classes of property.** There are now six different classes of property under the ACRS. Each of these classes reference old ADR lives and include the following personal property: three-year (special tools and racehorses); five-year (automobiles, computers, copiers, semiconductor manufacturing equipment, typewriters, etc.); seven-year (office furniture, fixtures and equipment, agricultural single-purpose buildings, etc.); 10-year (petroleum refining assets); 15-year (sewage treatment and telephone distribution plants); and 20-year (municipal sewers). A taxpayer can elect to use longer lives for the assets.

1) **Current methods applied.** The method prescribed for personal property is a 200% declining balance for three-year, five-year, seven-year, and 10-year property. The method prescribed for 15-year and 20-year personal property is the 150% declining balance method. However, taxpayers can elect to use the straight-line method to postpone deductions. In addition, a half-year convention is used for the year the property is placed in service or sold. Accordingly, only a half-year's deduction is allowed in the year the property is purchased or sold.

2) **Real property.** The recovery periods for real estate are 27.5 years for residential rental property and 39 years for other property.

3) **Recapture.** Present I.R.C. section 1250, applicable to buildings, allows recapture of only the difference between accelerated and straight-line depreciation as ordinary income. ACRS leaves this unchanged for residential real property and for nonresidential real property if straight-line depreciation was used. However, it requires the entire amount of prior depreciation to be recaptured as ordinary income if accelerated depreciation was used for nonresidential real property.

e. **Land.** Land is *not* depreciable since it has an unlimited useful life. Therefore, when a taxpayer purchases land and buildings he must allocate the purchase price between the buildings (which may be depreciated) and the land.

f. **Leaseholds.** The person who suffers due to a decrease in the value of property is entitled to claim the depreciation. This is generally the lessor, but there are exceptions, as when a lessee constructs a building on leased land (then the lessee may claim depreciation). For example, if a lessee is required to maintain property and return it to the lessor at the same value, the lessee would be entitled to deduct depreciation.

g. **Expensing.** I.R.C. section 179 allows taxpayers to expense up to $112,000 of personal business property placed in service in 2007. The $112,000 limitation is reduced dollar for dollar to the extent that total section 179 property placed in service during the tax year exceeds $450,000. The section 179 deduction is further limited to taxable income.

7. **Depletion.** I.R.C. section 611 allows the owner of a wasting asset (*e.g.,* oil, gas, minerals, gravel, timber, etc.) to deduct a reasonable allowance for its use or exploitation. A "wasting asset" is any deposit that is consumed by use or exploitation. There are two methods of computing depletion.

a. **Cost method.** The cost of the wasting asset is divided by the estimated number of units recoverable, to obtain a cost per unit. This figure is the deduction that may be claimed for each unit that is extracted. For example, if the total cost of drilling an oil well was $30 million and it is estimated that five million barrels of oil will be recovered from the well, the owner could claim a $6 depletion for each barrel of oil that is ultimately recovered.

 b. **Percentage method.** A fixed percentage of gross income may be deducted. Congress sets the percentage figure, which ranges from 5% (for gravel deposits) to 22% (for gas and oil). This method has the advantage of continued life, in contrast with cost depletion, which runs out when the cost of the asset is fully recovered.

  1) **Limitations.** Note that in no circumstance may this deduction exceed 50% of *net* income. The large oil companies are now precluded from using percentage depletion. Only the independents with no retail outlets or independents producing up to 1,000 barrels per day may use percentage depletion.

 c. **Intangible drilling costs.** The taxpayer has the option of either deducting intangible drilling costs or capitalizing them and then claiming depletion on their costs. [*See* I.R.C. §263(c)] The most advantageous method would be to deduct the costs and then to use the percentage depletion method, which is a percentage of gross income, not of cost.

8. **Application of Depreciation Rules.**

 a. **Property used for both business and pleasure--**

Sharp v. United States, 199 F. Supp. 743 (D. Del. 1961).

Facts. Hugh and Bayard Sharp bought a Beechcraft airplane for a total of $54,273.50. In taking allowed depreciation over the years, totaling $13,777.92, Hugh and Bayard acquiesced to a depreciation base that reflected the one to three ratio of business to personal use of the plane. When the plane was sold for $35,380 in 1954, the IRS required that the loss or gain be figured by using an adjusted business basis of $520.98 ($14,298.90 representing one-fourth of the cost minus the $13,777.92 allowed depreciation). Then the sale price was allocated to reflect the business-pleasure split, making $9,321.21 and $26,058.79 portions. By subtracting the adjusted basis from the allocated proceeds ($9,321.21 minus $520.98), the IRS came up with a figured gain of $8,800.23. As partners, Hugh and Bayard were each assessed with a $4,400.11 gain. They asserted that the adjusted basis to figure loss or gain should be computed by subtracting the depreciation allowed from the total cost without any allocation reflecting use ($54,273.50 - $13,772.92 = $40,495.58). This base, they contended, should be subtracted from the sale price ($35,380 minus $40,495.58) to arrive at a loss of $5,115.58 on the sale. They do not seek to deduct the loss; they claim only that no gain was realized. This is a ruling on cross-motions for summary judgments in the consolidated actions brought by Hugh and Bayard Sharp.

Issue. In figuring gain or loss on the sale of property used partly for business and partly for pleasure, must the cost basis and sale price be allocated to reflect the percentage of business use?

Held. Yes. Motion for summary judgment denied; government's motion granted.

♦ Loss or gain on the sale of property used partly for pleasure and partly for business must be allocated. This promotes uniformity and constitutes a long-accepted practice. It is similar to the practice of allocating the gain on sale of depreciable and nondepreciable property as a unit (*e.g.,* a building and land). The selling price is allocated between the two, and gain or loss is figured by referring to the adjusted basis of each.

♦ While it involves a fiction to divide an airplane, any other treatment would result in nonuniform tax treatment between those who use property exclusively for business purposes and those who use it also for pleasure.

---

b. Determinable useful life--

Simon v. Commissioner, 68 F.3d 41 (2d Cir. 1995).

Facts. In 1985, for $51,500 the Simons (Ps) purchased two violin bows made in the 19th century by a famous bow maker. The Tax Court found that old violins played with old bows produce exceptional sounds unmatched by new violins played with new bows. Old and new bows suffer wear and tear when used regularly and eventually become worn out, producing inferior sounds. Ps used the bows regularly in concerts and in rehearsals with the Philharmonic. Ps claimed an ACRS depreciation deduction for the bows on their 1989 Form 1040 in the amount of $10,815. Since the bows were collector's items, in spite of regular use the bows' value had actually increased to $80,000 by 1990. The IRS (D) disallowed the depreciation deduction, claiming that since the bows increased in value they did not have a determinable useful life. Ps claimed that under IRC section 168, recovery property is defined as tangible property subject to wear and tear used in a trade or business. Ps demonstrated that the bows did suffer wear and tear and that the bows were used regularly in Ps' trade or business. The Tax Court allowed the depreciation deduction. D appeals.

Issue. Can a tangible asset suffering wear and tear be depreciated even if the asset's determinable useful life cannot be determined?

Held. Yes. Judgment affirmed.

♦ Under the ACRS, "recovery property" means property subject to exhaustion, wear and tear, or obsolescence.

- Had the bows in question been held as an investment and not played, the bows would not have been depreciable. Because the bows were used regularly they were depreciable.

- Congress desired to stimulate investment in business generally through the ACRS methods, and it is not the court's function to distinguish between wasteful and productive business investment decisions.

- Under these rules, a law firm can purchase expensive antique desks and depreciate them under the ACRS even if the desks continue to appreciate in value.

Dissent. Ps have not established that the bows have determinable useful lives, thus the bows do not qualify for the depreciation deduction. I do not believe that Congress intended to abandon this concept.

D. DEDUCTIONS FOR PROFIT-MAKING, NONBUSINESS ACTIVITIES

1. **General Rule.** I.R.C. section 212 provides that an individual taxpayer is entitled to deduct expenses paid or incurred (i) for the production or collection of income; (ii) for the management, conservation, or maintenance of property held for the production of income; or (iii) in connection with the determination, collection, or refund of any tax.

2. **Effect.** The effect of section 212 is to give the individual investor the same types of deductions that a business has. The scope is substantially the same as I.R.C. section 162, which provides for "business expenses."

3. **Scope of Deductions Under Section 212.**

   a. **Personal investment activities--**

Higgins v. Commissioner, 312 U.S. 212 (1941).

Facts. Higgins (P) had extensive investments in real estate, stocks and bonds, etc. He spent a large portion of his time managing them and hired several people for that purpose. P had deducted salary and office expenses for 30 years, but the Commissioner (D) denied the deductions for 1932 and 1933. There was no dispute over whether these expenses were necessary and ordinary. The Commissioner admitted before the Board of Tax Appeals that the real estate activities in renting buildings were a business, and expenses related thereto were allowed as deductions. However, the Board held that P's investment activities with stocks and bonds did not constitute a business, but rather were personal investments. P argued that "elements of continuity, constant repetition, regularity and extent" differentiated his case from that of the small investor. The court of appeals affirmed, and P appeals.

Issue. Do personal investment activities of a taxpayer constitute carrying on a business for purposes of deducting expenses related thereto?

Held. No. Judgment affirmed.

♦ Whether management of personal investments constitutes "carrying on a business" depends on the facts of each case. Here, P and his staff merely kept records and collected dividends and interest from P's securities. No matter how continuous or extensive the work, these facts are not sufficient to reverse, as a matter of law, the determination of the Board.

Comment. The *Higgins* decision prompted Congress to enact I.R.C. section 212 (outlined *supra*). Therefore, the types of expenses involved in this case are now deductible.

---

b. Defending title to property--

Bowers v. Lumpkin, 140 F.2d 927 (4th Cir. 1944), *cert. denied*, 322 U.S. 755 (1944).

Facts. Lumpkin (P) was the beneficiary of a life interest in a testamentary trust that owned one-half of the stock in a corporation. She purchased the remaining stock from the trustees of an orphanage. During the years 1936 and 1937, she incurred substantial legal costs in defending her title against an attack by the Attorney General of South Carolina. She deducted these legal fees under the predecessor of I.R.C. section 212(2) as ordinary and necessary expenses incurred for the conservation of property held for the production of income. The Commissioner (D) disallowed the deductions, but the district court found for P.

Issue. May legal expenses incurred in defending title to property be deducted as "ordinary and necessary expenses" under I.R.C. section 212?

Held. No. Judgment reversed.

♦ Except for the requirement of being incurred in connection with a trade or business, section 212 deductions are subject to the same conditions as any other business deduction. It is well established, however, that legal fees incurred in defending legal title to property are not "ordinary and necessary" expenses. There is no evidence that Congress, in enacting section 212, intended to widen the scope of the phrase "ordinary and necessary." Thus, legal expenses incurred in defending or protecting title to property should be capitalized (*i.e.,* added to the cost of the property) and taken into account in computing the capital gain or loss on a subsequent sale.

♦ The word "conservation" in the predecessor to section 212 merely refers to expenses incurred in safeguarding property (*e.g.,* the cost of a safe deposit box for securities).

---

c. Proxy fights--

Surasky v. United States, 325 F.2d 191 (5th Cir. 1963).

Facts. Surasky (P), on the advice of Wolfson, purchased a large block of Montgomery Ward stock. Wolfson, who owned a much larger interest, was convinced that a change was needed in management. He accordingly organized a committee to get a new board of directors elected and force a sweeping change in management policies. P contributed $17,000 to the committee and deducted it as a nonbusiness expense. The committee's objectives were realized in part; during the next period dividends were increased, there was a stock split, and management policies were redirected. P then sold his stock for a substantial capital gain in addition to the substantial dividends already received. The Commissioner (D) disallowed the $17,000 deduction. The Tax Court upheld that decision on the grounds that there was no proximate relationship between the contribution and the production of income and that it was speculative whether the contribution would result in greater income.

Issue. Must a proximate relationship be shown between a deductible nonbusiness expense and the production of income or management of income-producing property?

Held. No. Judgment reversed and case remanded.

♦ There is nothing in the statute that requires a showing of a "proximate relation to the production . . . of taxable income." Congress rather had in mind allowing deduction for expenses genuinely incurred in the exercise of reasonable business judgment in an effort to produce income. Here, the payments, even if speculative, were made with the anticipation that increased profit would result. Since the expenses were incurred in the exercise of reasonable business judgment, the deduction should be allowed.

Comment. Revenue Ruling 64-236, issued following *Surasky*, indicated that the IRS will allow deductions for expenses for proxy fights if proximately related to the production or collection of income, or the management or conservation of income-producing property. However, the IRS refused to follow *Surasky* insofar as it does not require a proximate relationship.

---

d. Antenuptial agreements--

Meyer J. Fleischman v. Commissioner, 45 T.C. 439 (1966).

Facts. Meyer J. Fleischman got married in 1955. Before his marriage, he and his future wife entered into an antenuptial agreement whereby she would, in the event of divorce, relinquish all claims to his property in exchange for $5,000. In 1961, the wife sued for divorce and in a separate action sued to have the antenuptial agreement set aside. The second suit was dismissed with prejudice. On his 1962 return, Fleischman did not deduct the costs of the divorce suit, but he did deduct $3,000 for legal expenses of defending the other suit. The Commissioner disallowed the deduction and assessed a deficiency. Fleischman argues that these expenses were caused by a separate suit to rescind a contract, not by the divorce proceeding, and that they were incurred to preserve and protect real property inherited from his mother.

Issue. Are legal expenses incurred in a suit to set aside an antenuptial agreement deductible?

Held. No. Commissioner's determination upheld.

◆ Legal expenses incurred in a suit to set aside an antenuptial agreement are not deductible because they flow from the marriage relationship and not from a profit-seeking relationship. In this case, while the suit to set aside the petitioner's antenuptial agreement concerned contract rights, it was intimately bound up with the divorce litigation. Thus, the expenses incurred were personal in nature, specifically nondeductible under I.R.C. section 262.

◆ The "origin of the claim" test is used because it is most consistent with the meaning of I.R.C. section 23(a)(2). Under this test, expenses to preserve and protect income-producing property in a divorce proceeding are not deductible because they are a personal expense arising out of the marital relationship.

◆ Legal expenses incurred by a spouse in securing alimony are, however, deductible because alimony is taxable income and the law provides that legal expenses incurred to produce taxable income are deductible.

4. **Losses on Residential Property.** As a general rule, losses on the sale of a personal residence are not deductible. However, this rule is subject to the qualifications set out in the cases below.

a. **Rental requirement--**

William C. Horrmann v. Commissioner, 17 T.C. 903 (1951).

Facts. William C. Horrmann acquired a house at 189 Howard Avenue in New York by devise from his mother. Within the year, he redecorated it and moved in. Shortly thereafter, he sold his former residence. Two years later, he abandoned the Howard Avenue house, complaining that it was too expensive and too large. He considered converting it to apartments, but found that impractical. He made several attempts to sell or rent the property. Finally, almost five years after acquiring the property, he sold it for net proceeds of $20,800. The house had been worth $60,000 when acquired, and was worth $45,000 when sold. Horrmann contends that he is entitled to depreciation deductions for 1943, 1944, and 1945; that he is entitled to a deduction for maintenance expense for that period; and that he is entitled to a deduction for a long-term capital loss from the sale.

Issues. On a building once used as a residence but later offered for rent or sale:

     (i)   Can depreciation deductions be taken?

     (ii)   May a taxpayer deduct expenses incurred for maintenance and conservation of the property?

     (iii)   May a taxpayer deduct a long-term capital loss arising from the sale of such property?

Held. (i) Yes. (ii) Yes. (iii) No.

♦   The language of the I.R.C. is "property held for the production of income," and the owner's use of the property along with his future intended use are generally controlling. When efforts are made to rent the property, it is being held for production of income and the depreciation deductions should be allowed.

♦   For maintenance and conservation, the same issues as in the above paragraph are controlling, and hence deductions for maintenance and conservation of the property should be allowed.

♦   The controlling language of the I.R.C. on the issue of long-term capital loss is "in any transaction entered into for profit." When property has been used as a personal residence, in order to convert the transaction into one entered into for profit, the owner must do more than just abandon the property and list it for sale or rent. If he actually rents it, his decision to convert the property to income-producing property is irrevocable for the term of the lease. But if he only instructs an agent to sell the property, the change of character remains subject to his will, since he can revoke the agency at any time. Thus, it would strain the language of the regulations to say that such property was "appropriated to" or "used for" income producing purposes. Previous cases that have held that actual rental was not necessary involved different facts, where the owners had inherited the property and never intended to occupy it as a personal residence.

b. Taxpayer's intention--

Lowry v. United States, 384 F. Supp. 257 (D.N.H. 1974).

Facts. Lowry (P) owned property on Martha's Vineyard that he had used as a summer home for many years. It was subject to restrictive covenants requiring the approval of 75% of the other owners in order to resell or rent for more than a year. In 1966, P bought a house in New Hampshire and decided he no longer needed the Martha's Vineyard home. At that time, the house was worth about $50,000, but P believed that a real estate boom in the late 1960s, with inflation, would push the value up to his asking price of $150,000. The house was never used again, except that each spring P would open the house and clean it, and each fall he would close it, each time spending two or three days there. P did not try to rent the house because he felt it would be easier to sell an empty, clean house and because he did not want the expense of furnishing household items. When P's daughter returned from Europe and asked to use the property, P refused, saying that the property was a business proposition, and rented her a house in Maine. In 1968, someone offered the right price, but approval of the other owners could not be obtained. In 1973, P succeeded in selling the property for $150,000 cash. P showed a $100,536.50 net long-term capital gain on his tax return for 1973. P deducted maintenance expenses for five years, and the Commissioner (D) challenged those deductions for 1970 only.

Issue. Is residential property converted into income-producing property if it is abandoned and offered for sale, but not rent, with a reasonable expectation of profit?

Held. Yes. Judgment for P.

- ◆ The rule once was that premises must be offered for rent in order to have maintenance expenses deductible on a personal residence. But in *Frank A. Newcombe*, 54 T.C. 1298 (1970), the court found the key question to be "the intention of the taxpayer in light of all the facts and circumstances." In determining whether the taxpayer intended to obtain a profit, the following were important considerations: (i) the length of time the taxpayer occupied the former residence prior to abandonment, (ii) the availability of the house for the taxpayer's personal use while it was unoccupied, (iii) the recreational character of the house, (iv) attempts to rent the property, and (v) whether the offer to sell was an attempt to realize postconversion appreciation.

- ◆ In this case, P had had extensive experience in the real estate market. He reasonably believed that he would be able to realize the asking price on the real estate within a few years, and during the interim he carefully treated the property as a "business proposition." Thus, in light of all the circumstances, it is clear that P intended to convert his property into income-producing property and benefit from post-abandonment appreciation.

E. DEDUCTIONS NOT LIMITED TO BUSINESS OR PROFIT-SEEKING ACTIVITIES

1. **Interest.** I.R.C. section 163 allows the taxpayer to deduct certain interest payments. Prior to the Tax Reform Act of 1986, all interest (both personal and business) was deductible. However, beginning in 1987, the only personal interest that was deductible was home mortgage interest. Other personal interest was phased out over a four-year period ending in 1990. Recently, section 221 was added to allow a deduction for "personal" interest on "qualified education loans." This deduction is phased out ratably for single taxpayers with adjusted gross income over $50,000 and for married taxpayers with adjusted gross income over $100,000. Home mortgage interest is now limited to interest on acquisition debt limited to $1 million of debt, and up to an additional $100,000 in home equity debt. Mortgages on a principal and one additional residence can qualify for qualified mortgage interest.

   a. **What is interest?** Payments for the use of money qualify as interest. These could be thought of as rental payments for the use of money. Conversely, service charges for the lender's services are not deductible as interest.

      1) **Points.** Some lenders charge an additional "loan processing fee" (points) when loaning money. These charges are considered payments for the use of money and are deductible as interest. [Rev. Rul. 69-188, 1969-1 C.B. 54]

   b. **Limitations.** Interest incurred in a trade or business will be fully deductible. Interest incurred in acquiring investments will be deductible only to the extent of net investment income. Home mortgage interest will be deductible on a first and second residence. However, the debt cannot exceed the original cost of the property plus improvements. Taxpayers can obtain second mortgages (subject to the limitations) and pay off nondeductible personal loans. In addition, the second mortgage loan proceeds can be used to purchase other personal items.

   c. **Requirements for deductibility.**

      1) **Debt of taxpayer.** The indebtedness must be owed by the taxpayer, not someone else, but the taxpayer need not be personally liable on the loan.

      2) **Bona fide debt.** The transaction must have economic substance.

         a) **Shams.** A mere paper transaction does not give rise to an interest deduction.

         b) **No change in beneficial interest.** A transaction must affect the taxpayer's beneficial interest to raise an interest deduction.

That is, the transaction must have a reasonable possibility of producing gain or loss.

    c)   **Business purpose.** Interest is not deductible unless the taxpayer had some purpose other than (or along with) tax saving in incurring the debt.

    d)   **Family loans.** Interest on debts between family members is not disallowed, but the courts are careful to determine that there is indeed a bona fide debt.

    e)   **Interest or dividends.** Sometimes investors in a close corporation will seek to minimize their investment in stock, which pays them nondeductible dividends. Instead, they will "lend" the corporation money and receive interest (in lieu of dividends) which the corporation can deduct. The courts have recharacterized many of these loans as contributions to capital. This changes the interest payments to dividends. In determining whether debt is really equity, the courts look at the corporation's ratio of debt to equity. A ratio of four (debt) to one (equity) is considered "safe."

  d.   **Interest disallowed.**

    1)   **Tax-exempt interest.** I.R.C. section 265(c) does not allow the deduction of interest paid on money borrowed to purchase tax-exempt state or municipal bonds.

    2)   **Construction period interest and taxes.** Interest and taxes on property under construction are not deductible. They must be capitalized and deducted over an amortization period provided by statute.

  e.   **Imputed interest on low-interest loans.**

    1)   **Former rule--**

J. Simpson Dean v. Commissioner, 35 T.C. 1083 (1961).

Facts. The Deans owned a corporation, which lent them about $2 million in exchange for interest-free notes. The Commissioner alleged that the interest on these notes (at the prime rate) was income to the Deans. The Deans brought suit to set aside the assessment on the grounds that interest-free loans do not yield taxable income and are not a substitute for dividend distributions.

Issue. Does an interest-free loan from a controlled corporation to officers of that corporation result in taxable income to the officers?

Held. No. Deficiency set aside.

◆   An interest-free loan does not result in the realization of income to the debtor. Even if the Deans had paid interest, that interest would have been fully deductible. It is illogical to impute income where a deduction would have been allowed.

◆   This is not the same as using corporate property rent-free. The officer would not have been able to claim a deduction if he had acquired that property personally.

◆   If the Deans are able to use the money to create other income, that income will be taxable.

Concurrence. The interest deductions would not necessarily have equaled the interest payments. Even if they had, that does not necessarily mean that there was no income. To hold that interest-free loans produce no income is too broad. The majority should have limited its holding to a ruling of no deficiency.

Dissent. Interest in the sense that it represents compensation paid for the use, forbearance, or detention of money may be likened to "rent," which is paid for the use of property. It is hard to believe that there was no economic benefit to the Deans in being able to borrow $2 million without any obligation to pay interest.

Comment. The I.R.C. now *imputes* interest in all interest-free or no-interest loans (*see* below), eliminating the tax advantage of the type of transaction involved in *Dean*.

---

2)   **Current law.** I.R.C. section 7872, from the Tax Reform Act of 1984, contains rules to impute interest on below-market interest loans. Depending on the character of the loan, a transfer of income, dividend, gift, contribution to capital, or compensation is imputed from the lender to the borrower, and in turn a retransfer to the lender is imputed.

        a)   **Gift loan.** The lender realizes interest income for the year, based on the applicable federal rate; the borrower can claim an interest payment deduction for the same amount.

                (1)   **Term loan.** If the loan is for a specific term, the present value of the principal as well as the first-year interest is taxed in the year the loan was made. Therefore, interest income is recognized before interest is deductible.

                (2)   **Demand loan.** If the loan is payable on demand, the imputed interest is the difference between actual interest

payments and the amount that would be payable using the applicable federal rate. This calculation is made each year the loan is outstanding. Demand loans result in offsetting interest income and deductions each year.

(3) Exception. Section 7872 applies only when the aggregate amount of loans between individuals is greater than $10,000. This de minimis exception applies if the loans are not for purchase of income-producing property. Also, if the aggregate loan is not more than $100,000, the amount of imputed interest for both individuals is limited to the borrower's net investment income for the year; if income does not exceed $1,000, no interest is imputed.

b) Nongift loans. The imputed interest of a nongift loan is characterized as a dividend (if between company and stockholder), compensation (if between employee and employer or contractor and client), or interest (if tax-avoidance or other below-market interest loan).

(1) The rules for calculating imputed interest on demand and term nongift loans are the same as for gift loans.

(2) The same $10,000 de minimis exception as for gift loans applies to compensation-related or corporate-shareholder loans, but not to tax-avoidance loans.

2. Taxes.

a. Introduction. I.R.C. section 164 allows every taxpayer to deduct various kinds of state and local taxes, including income taxes, real and personal property taxes, and gasoline taxes. Also, a taxpayer may deduct certain taxes paid in connection with his business or investment, which would otherwise not be deductible. These include excise taxes and Social Security taxes paid on employees. However, certain types of taxes are never deductible. These include federal income taxes, federal estate and gift taxes, and state inheritance taxes.

b. Deductible real estate taxes--

Cramer v. Commissioner, 55 T.C. 1125 (1971).

Facts. Cramer (P) sold real property (property #1) under a land sale contract. Thus, P retained legal title to property #1. During 1964 and 1965, the purchaser failed to pay the real property taxes. Consequently, P paid the taxes and instituted a foreclosure suit.

In 1966, P took possession of property #1. Later in 1966, P resold property #1. Also during 1965 and 1966, P paid real property taxes on her ailing mother's residence (property #2). Finally, P purchased a new residence (property #3) and paid taxes on the property through an escrow agent. In 1964, 1965, and 1966, P deducted all the taxes paid on properties #1, #2, and #3. The Commissioner (D) allowed the deductions for property #3, but disallowed the others.

Issue. Are taxes paid on property #1 and property #2 deductible?

Held. Yes as to property #1; no as to property #2.

♦ Although P sold property #1, she retained legal title and was liable for the taxes under state law. Therefore, the taxes were deductible to P under Treasury Regulation 1.164-1(a) as the one on whom they were imposed. However, only a portion of the 1966 taxes were deductible since P resold the property during the year. [Rev. Rul. 67-31, 1967-1 C.B. 49]

♦ P was not the owner of property #2. Consequently, the taxes were not imposed on P. Therefore, P was not entitled to claim a deduction for the taxes paid.

F. RESTRICTIONS ON DEDUCTIONS

1. **Artificial Losses.**

   a. **"At risk" limitation.** I.R.C. section 465(a) sharply limits the current deduction of operating losses from certain investments to the amount that the taxpayer has "at risk" in the investment.

      1) **Definition of "at risk."** The term means the amount of the taxpayer's investment in the property, but not counting purchase-money loans for which the taxpayer has no personal liability.

      2) **Activities covered.** I.R.C. section 465(c)(3) provides that the "at risk rules" apply to "each activity engaged in by the taxpayer in carrying on a trade or business or for the production of income." Prior to the Tax Reform Act of 1986, real estate was exempt from the at risk rules. Beginning in 1987, taxpayers are no longer at risk with respect to real estate if they obtain nonrecourse financing from someone other than a third-party financial institution.

      3) **Definition of operating loss.** "Losses" are the excess of deductions from the activity over income from the activity during the year.

b. **Hobby losses.** A taxpayer may only deduct the losses of a ***profit-seeking activity***. An activity is presumed to be for profit-seeking purposes if for at least three of the last five taxable years, the activity brought the taxpayer a net profit. Otherwise, the facts and circumstances are explored to ascertain the taxpayer's intent. If it is found that the losses were sustained in a nonprofit-seeking activity (such as a hobby), the taxpayer may deduct only interest, taxes, and other costs not to exceed the income produced from the investment.

2. **Other Restrictions on Deductions.**

a. **Restrictions on home deductions.** I.R.C. section 280A provides that the allowable deductions associated with a dwelling used as a personal residence are limited to those otherwise deductible. These would include interest, maintenance expenses, and property taxes. Use as a personal residence is defined as personal use of the unit, the greater of 14 days or 10% of the days it is rented. To illustrate the allocation rules of I.R.C. section 280A, assume these facts for the following examples: The taxpayer rented a vacation home for 91 days and occupied it for personal use for 32 days for a total of 121 days used. Interest and taxes were $3,475 and maintenance costs were $2,693. Rental income is $2,700.

   1) **Maintenance costs.** I.R.C. section 280A(c)(3) further allows deduction of maintenance expense attributable to the rental of the unit. The amount deductible is the pro rata portion attributable to days rented vis-a-vis total days the unit was used. In this example, the deductible portion of the maintenance expense would be:

      91 days rented/121 total days used × $2,693 = $2,020

   2) **Limitation.** I.R.C. section 280A(c)(5) provides that the deduction allocable to the rental of the unit (including interest, taxes, and maintenance) cannot exceed the rental income from the unit. Interest and taxes are allocated according to the number of days rented divided by 365. In this example, the interest ($2,854) and taxes ($621) of $3,475 allocable to the rental portion is:

      91 days rented/365 × $3,475 = $868

   3) **Example.** The above two calculations show the amount of deductible maintenance expense to be:

$2,700	gross income
- 868	allocable interest and taxes
$1,832	of $2,020 maintenance expense deductible.

b. **Passive activity limitations.**

1) **General rule.** I.R.C. section 469 limits deductions from passive activities to income from such activities. A passive activity is one where the taxpayer does not "materially participate" in the conduct of the trade or business. All limited partnership interests are passive investments. In addition, property held for rent is defined to be passive. All of the taxpayer's passive activities are combined and tested for net passive income or loss. Passive losses can be carried forward indefinitely.

2) **Taxpayer subject to the limitations.** The passive loss rules apply to individuals, estates and trusts, closely held C corporations, and personal service corporations. Conduit entities such as partnerships and S corporations are not subject to the passive loss rules. However, the shareholders and partners are subject to the rules.

3) **Exception.** Individuals who actively participate in real estate rental activities can deduct up to $25,000 net passive losses attributable to such activities. However, the $25,000 amount is phased out for taxpayers with adjusted gross incomes between $100,000 and $150,000.

3. **Illegality or Impropriety.**

a. **Wagering.** Since wagering is a profit-seeking activity, losses are deductible, but only to the extent of wagering gains.

b. **Bribes or kickbacks.** No deduction is allowed for any bribe, kickback, or payment to a government official or employee. Bribes and kickbacks to those outside the government are also not deductible if their illegality can be established by criminal law or by statute that subjects the violator to loss of a license or privilege of doing business. Also, as to the latter category, the IRS must show that the law is generally enforced.

c. **Fines.** No deduction is allowed for the payment of any fine or penalty to the government (federal, state, or local) for the violation of any law.

d. **Legal expenses in defending against criminal prosecution--**

Commissioner v. Tellier, 383 U.S. 687 (1966).

Facts. Tellier was in the business of underwriting the public sale of stock offerings and purchasing securities for resale to customers. He was brought to trial and convicted of violating the fraud section of the Securities Act of 1933 and the mail fraud statute, and with conspiring to violate those statutes. In his defense he paid $22,964.20 in legal expenses. He claimed a deduction for that amount on his federal income tax return. The Commissioner disallowed the deduction, and the Commissioner's decision was sustained by the Tax Court. The Court of Appeals for the Second Circuit reversed. The Supreme Court granted certiorari.

Issue. Are expenses incurred by a taxpayer in the unsuccessful defense of a criminal prosecution deductible as ordinary and necessary business expenses?

Held. Yes. Judgment of court of appeals affirmed.

♦   There is no doubt that the payments deducted by Tellier were ordinary and necessary expenses of his security business, and the Commissioner does not contend otherwise.

♦   Nevertheless, the Commissioner and the Tax Court found that the deduction should be disallowed on public policy grounds. No public policy is offended when a man faced with serious criminal charges employs a lawyer to help in his defense. That is not "proscribed conduct." It is his constitutional right.

G.   DEDUCTIONS FOR INDIVIDUALS ONLY

1.   **Moving Expenses.** I.R.C. section 217 allows an employee or self-employed individual to deduct as an adjustment to gross income expenses incurred in moving himself and his family. Eligible expenses are limited to transportation of household goods and personal effects and travel (excluding meals) to the new residence. To qualify, the new job site must be over 50 miles further from the old home than the old job site was.

2.   **Adjusted Gross Income.** Review section I.E.1. of this outline, *supra*, to recall that adjusted gross income is equal to *gross income* less *deductions for trade or business expenses*.

3.   **Extraordinary Medical Expenses.** I.R.C. section 213 provides a limited deduction for amounts paid "for the diagnosis, cure, mitigation, treatment, or prevention of a disease, or for the purpose of affecting any structure or function of the body."

   a.   **Limitations on amount deductible.** Only expenses in excess of 7½% of adjusted gross income are deductible. This includes amounts spent for prescription drugs.

   b.   **Capital improvements--**

Raymon Gerard v. Commissioner, 37 T.C. 826 (1962).

Facts. Raymon Gerard's daughter suffered from cystic fibrosis, a disease that requires special diets, treatment with antibiotics, and strict environmental controls. Gerard installed a room air conditioner in his daughter's room so that she would not be exposed to dry, dusty air, but her being confined to one room all day was felt to be psychologically damaging. Accordingly, Gerard installed a central unit for the whole house. The unit cost $1,300 and increased the value of the home by $800. Gerard deducted the $1,300 as a medical expense. The Commissioner disallowed it, and this petition was brought.

Issue. Is the cost of a capital improvement to property for medical reasons deductible in its entirety?

Held. No. $500 deduction allowed.

♦ Normally, the entire cost of medical care is deductible under I.R.C. section 213. However, section 263(a)(1) provides that "no deduction shall be allowed for 'any amount paid out' for permanent improvement or betterments made to increase the value of any property."

♦ Thus, when the medical care expenditure is for a permanent addition to the taxpayer's home, deductibility as a medical expense depends on whether it increases the value of the home. The theory is that an increase in property value is compensation for the expense of the improvement. It follows logically that where the increase in value is less than the expenditure, the difference should be deductible as a medical expense. Accordingly, Gerard may deduct $500.

---

c. **Weight loss program costs.** Revenue Ruling 2002-19 involved the deductibility of the costs of participating in a weight-loss program as treatment for a specific disease (including obesity) that had been diagnosed by a doctor. A taxpayer was diagnosed by a doctor as being obese. Another taxpayer was not obese, but was diagnosed with hypertension and directed to lose weight as treatment for the hypertension. Both taxpayers joined a weight-loss program. They both paid an initial fee to join the program and additional fees to attend periodic meetings. At the meetings, they developed diet plans and worked out problems encountered in dieting. They also purchased the program's diet food. None of the diet costs were compensated by insurance. The IRS held that the costs of participating in a weight-loss program are deductible medical expenses under I.R.C. section 213 if the individual is directed to lose weight by a physician for treatment of a specific disease. However, the cost of diet foods is not deductible since these foods are substitutes for the food the taxpayers normally consume. Obesity is a medically accepted disease. Weight-loss program costs incurred for improving appearance, general health, and sense of well-being, and not to cure a specific disease or ailment, are not deductible medical expenses.

d. Cosmetic surgery excluded. I.R.C. section 213(d)(9) now excludes cosmetic surgery or similar procedures from the definition of medical care unless such procedure is necessary because of a deformity from injury, disease, or congenital abnormality.

4. **Qualified Tuition and Related Expenses.** Starting for the years after 2001, an individual can take an above-the-line deduction for qualified tuition and related expenses. Qualified expenses are the costs of enrollment or attendance at an eligible educational institution of higher education for a person who is the taxpayer or the spouse or dependent of the taxpayer. There are a variety of limitations on this deduction.

5. **Personal Exemptions.** A taxpayer may deduct $3,400 in 2007 for each exemption for which she qualifies under I.R.C. sections 151 through 154. The amount is adjusted each year for inflation.

   a. Personal. Generally, a taxpayer may always claim an exemption for herself. She may also claim additional exemptions for being over 65 and/or blind. The taxpayer's spouse may claim these same exemptions if a joint return is filed.

   b. Dependents. An additional exemption may be claimed for each "dependent" who meets certain qualifications. However, an individual claimed as a dependent by another taxpayer is not entitled to the exemption.

      1) **Gross income test.** The dependent's gross income must be less than the exemption amount unless he is under 19 or a student. [I.R.C. §151(e)]

      2) **Support test.** The taxpayer must supply over one-half of the dependent's support. [I.R.C. §152(a)]

      3) **Relationship test.** The dependent must either be a close relative of the taxpayer or have his principal place of residence with the taxpayer. [I.R.C. §152(a)]

   c. Special rules.

      1) **Multiple support agreement.** If several people all contribute to the dependent's support (for example, four children each contributing 25% of their mother's support), any one of them can claim the exemption pursuant to a multiple support agreement. Such an agreement will allocate the exemption to one of the contributors, often rotating it from year to year.

      2) **Divorced parents.** A frequent problem is determining which of the divorced parents is entitled to exemptions for the children.

a) As a general rule, the exemption is given to the parent who has custody.

b) The noncustodial parent gets the exemption if the custodial parent signs a written release of her right to claim the exemption for the current year. The noncustodial parent must attach the declaration to his return. This permission allows the parents to negotiate over who gets the exemption and to compensate the parent who does not claim it.

c) The law prior to 1984, under which the exemption could be allocated to the noncustodial parent by a divorce decree or a written agreement, remains applicable to pre-1985 decrees or agreements (unless the spouses modified these agreements after 1984, explicitly adopting the new provisions).

6. **Standard Deduction.** Once adjusted gross income has been determined, the taxpayer has the option of either: (i) itemizing the deductions from adjusted gross income (*supra*), or (ii) claiming the standard deduction. The latter option is usually more advantageous to the wage earner who does not own a mortgaged home, make extensive contributions, or otherwise have a large number of deductions from adjusted gross income. For the taxable year 2006, the standard deduction was $10,300 on a joint return, $7,550 for a head of household, and $5,150 for unmarried individuals. These amounts are increased yearly for inflation. The standard deduction is also increased by a set amount if the taxpayer is 65 years of age or blind ($1,250 for an unmarried person, $1,000 for a married taxpayer).

a. **Contingent-fee agreement--**

Commissioner v. Banks, 543 U.S. 426, 125 S. Ct. 826 (2005).

Facts. Two cases were consolidated for review by the Supreme Court. One was *Banks v. Commissioner*, 345 F.3d 373 (2003). In this case, after Banks (D1) was fired from his job as an educational consultant, he retained an attorney, signed a contingent-fee agreement, and filed a civil suit against his employer, alleging employment discrimination in violation of the Civil Rights Act of 1964. The parties settled for $464,000. D1 paid $150,000 of this amount to his attorney pursuant to the fee agreement.

The other case was *Banaitis v. Commissioner*, 340 F.3d 1074 (2003). In this case, Banaitis (D2) left his job as a vice president and loan officer at a bank and subsequently retained an attorney on a contingent-fee basis and sued the bank. D2 alleged that the bank had willfully interfered with his employment contract, had attempted to induce him to breach his fiduciary duties to customers, and had discharged him when he refused. After a jury trial, D2 was awarded compensatory and punitive damages.

After all appeals and post-trial motions were resolved, the parties settled. The bank paid $4,864,547 to D2. Pursuant to the formula set forth in the contingent fee contract, the bank paid an additional $3,864,012 directly to D2's attorney.

Neither D1 nor D2 included attorney's fees as gross income on his federal income tax return. The Commissioner of Internal Revenue (P) issued a notice of deficiency to each of them, which the Tax Court upheld. In D1's case, the court of appeals reversed in part, finding that the amount D1 paid to his attorney was not includable as gross income. In D2's case, the court of appeals found that because Oregon law grants attorneys a superior lien in the contingent-fee portion of any recovery, that part of D2's settlement was not includable as gross income. The Supreme Court granted certiorari.

Issue. For federal income tax purposes, when a litigant's recovery of a money judgment or settlement constitutes gross income under section 61(a) of the Internal Revenue Code (26 U.S.C. §61(a)), does gross income include that portion of the recovery paid to the attorney as a contingent fee?

Held. Yes. Judgment reversed and cases remanded.

♦ The issue is important because the Alternative Minimum Tax establishes a tax liability floor and does not allow taking the legal expenses as miscellaneous itemized deductions. Also, the American Jobs Creation Act of 2004 amended the IRS Code to allow a taxpayer to deduct attorney's fees, such as the fees involved here, in computing adjusted gross income. However, that amendment does not apply here because it was passed after these cases arose and is not retroactive.

♦ "Gross income" is broadly defined to include all gains not otherwise exempted. A taxpayer cannot eliminate an economic gain from gross income by assigning it in advance to another party, because gains should be taxed "to those who earn them." The anticipatory assignment of income doctrine is intended to stop taxpayers from avoiding taxation by means of arrangements and contracts created to prevent income from vesting in the person who earned it. The rule is preventative and is motivated by administrative and substantive concerns. This Court does not ask whether any particular assignment has a discernible tax avoidance purpose.

♦ P contends that a contingent-fee agreement should be viewed as an anticipatory assignment to the attorney of a part of the client's income from any litigation recovery. In order to determine attribution of income, the question is whether a taxpayer exercises complete dominion over the income at issue. However, in the case of anticipatory assignments, where the assignor may not have dominion over the income at the moment of receipt, the question is whether the assignor retains dominion over the income-generating asset. This preserves the principle that income should be taxed to the party who earns it and enjoys the consequent benefits.

♦   The income-generating asset is the cause of action that stems from a plaintiff's injury in the case of litigation recovery. We reject Ds' argument that because the recovery value is speculative at the time of assignment, the anticipatory assignment doctrine does not apply. Nor do we accept Ds' argument that the attorney-client relationship be treated as a business partnership or joint venture for tax purposes. While the attorney can make tactical decisions alone, the client determines whether the case proceeds to trial or is settled, and he makes additional critical decisions. The attorney is an agent duty-bound to act in the principal's interest, and the client retains dominion and control over the underlying claim. Thus, it is appropriate to treat the total recovery as income to the principal. Even where state law confers special rights or protection on the attorney, as long as the basic relationship of principal-agent is not changed, this rule applies.

Comment. In cases where attorney fees are greater than damages, such as in public interest litigation where relief is injunctive or awards are minimal, a plaintiff could be forced to pay more in taxes than he won in the award. After the plaintiff has paid the IRS, then the IRS gets a second bite of the apple by taxing the income received by the attorney.

V. THE YEAR OF INCLUSION OR DEDUCTION

A. INTRODUCTION

This chapter deals with the problems that arise in assigning particular elements of income or deductions to a particular tax year. The question of when income is taxed depends on two factors.

1. **Taxpayer's Method of Accounting.** There are two basic methods of accounting—the *cash method* and the *accrual method*. Under the cash method, income is recognized when "received" and deductions are recognized when "paid." Under the accrual method, income is recognized when "earned" and deductions are recognized when "incurred." Most individuals and small businesses use the cash method, while most corporations use the accrual method. The Commissioner is given broad authority to ensure that the taxpayer's method "clearly reflects income" and to permit or refuse accounting changes and even select an accounting method for the taxpayer. The Tax Reform Act of 1986 requires corporate and certain other taxpayers with annual gross receipts in excess of $5 million to use the accrual method of accounting.

2. **Selecting the Tax Year.** The second factor is in what year the taxpayer's income is taxed and deductions permitted. The year in which income will be taxed is important for numerous reasons. From one year to the next, tax law, tax rates, or a taxpayer's filing status may change. Also, a taxpayer can avoid higher tax rates if she can spread her income over more than one year. Finally, deferring income into a later year or accelerating deductions into an earlier year will delay the payment of tax.

B. METHODS OF ACCOUNTING

I.R.C. section 446 provides that taxpayers shall compute taxable income under the method of accounting on the basis of which the taxpayer regularly computes her income in keeping her books. However, the method must "clearly reflect income."

1. **Cash Method.** When the cash method is used, income is recognized when it is "received" and deductions are taken when "paid." A cash-basis taxpayer may in some instances materially affect her net income by accelerating or postponing receipt of income or payment of expenses.

   a. **Receipts.**

      1) **Receiving the check--**

Charles F. Kahler v. Commissioner, 18 T.C. 31 (1952).

Facts. Kahler received a check after banking hours on December 31, 1946. He argued that receipt of a check should not give rise to income unless the check was received in time to convert it to cash before the end of the taxable year. The Commissioner determined that the check should be included in income for 1946. Kahler petitioned the court.

Issue. Does the cash-basis taxpayer realize income on the date he receives a check if he receives it after banking hours?

Held. Yes. Judgment for Commissioner.

♦ The tax regulations provide that when services are compensated by something other than money, the fair market value of the property received is taken into income. Thus, it is irrelevant whether or not the check was *immediately* cashable.

♦ The law of negotiable instruments provides that once a check is presented and honored, the date of payment relates back to the time of delivery.

♦ As a practical matter, most people think of payment by check as the virtual equivalent of cash.

Concurrence. There was another bank in town that might have been open. Furthermore, Kahler might have been able to cash the check at a market, or he might have used it to discharge some obligation during 1946.

2) Unsecured promissory note--

Williams v. Commissioner, 28 T.C. 1000 (1957).

Facts. Jay Williams (P) was a cash-basis taxpayer who performed services for McConkey and Housley during 1951. At the time of completing the services, P received an unsecured, noninterest-bearing promissory note in the amount of $7,166.60, payable 240 days thereafter. It was clear at the time of issuance that the maker would be unable to pay anything on the note in the near future. P tried on 10 or 15 occasions to sell the note to various banks, but was unsuccessful. In 1954, P received $6,666.66 from Housley as payment in full on the note. P reported the amount received as income in 1954. The Commissioner determined that the receipt of the note constituted taxable income of $7,166.60 in 1951.

Issue. Does the receipt of a note as an evidence of indebtedness, not as payment of the outstanding debt, constitute income at the time of receipt?

Held. No. Judgment for P.

♦ The note in question was not received as payment of the outstanding debt owed to P for the performance of his services, but merely as evidence of the indebtedness. It had no fair market value and P knew at the time of receipt that the maker would be unable to pay off the note until a much later date. A simple change in the form of indebtedness from an accounts payable to a note payable is not equivalent to a cash receipt that would be currently realizable as income. Thus, we hold that receipt by P of the promissory note in 1951 did not constitute taxable realized income during that year.

---

3) Cash equivalency doctrine--

Cowden v. Commissioner, 289 F.2d 20 (5th Cir. 1961).

Facts. In April 1951, Cowden (P), his wife, and their children executed an oil and gas lease on P's land to Stanolind Oil Co. Stanolind agreed to pay P and his family $511,192 in royalties, $10,224 payable on execution, $250,484 payable in January 1952, and $250,484 payable in January 1953. Instruments were drawn up, and P assigned them to a bank of which he was a director. The bank discounted the obligations at 4% and paid P the difference. The Commissioner (D) determined that $487,647 should be taxed as ordinary income in 1951. P brought suit in Tax Court, which held the entire $511,192 taxable in 1941. P appeals.

Issue. If a promise to pay is the equivalent of cash, is it taxable as if cash had actually been received?

Held. Yes. Judgment affirmed.

♦ If a promise to pay of a solvent obligor is unconditional and assignable, not subject to setoffs, and is of a kind that is frequently transferred to lenders or investors, such promise is the equivalent of cash and taxable as cash would have been taxed had it been received by the taxpayer.

♦ If a consideration for which one of the parties bargains is the equivalent of cash, it will be subjected to taxation to the extent of its fair market value.

---

4) **Constructive receipt.** If a cash-basis taxpayer has an ***unqualified right*** to money or property ***plus*** the power to obtain it, it is thought to be so much within his control as to be equivalent to his actually receiving it. Thus, he "constructively received" the money or property.

a) Unfettered control by recipient--

Hornung v. Commissioner, 47 T.C. 428 (1967).

Facts. Hornung was selected the most valuable player of the National Football League championship game in December 1961. As a result, he won a car, which was delivered on January 3, 1962. Hornung argued that the car was income to him in 1961 since the donor of the car, *Sport Magazine*, said that the car was available to him on December 31, 1961. The Commissioner assessed a deficiency, which Hornung paid before filing suit for a refund.

Issue. Did the taxpayer have sufficient control over the car in 1961 to constitute a constructive receipt?

Held. No. Judgment for Commissioner.

♦ The basis of constructive receipt is unfettered control by the recipient before the date of actual receipt. On December 31, 1961, the car was in the possession of the Chevrolet dealer, and *Sport Magazine* had neither title nor the keys to the car. Hornung has failed to show that he possessed any control over the car at year's end.

♦ The doctrine of constructive receipt was conceived to prevent a taxpayer from arbitrarily choosing the year in which he will recognize income by deciding when to reduce the income to his possession.

Comment. Note that the operation of this provision is ***mandatory***, even if it works to the advantage of the taxpayer. *Kahler, supra*, also illustrates the concept of constructive receipt.

---

b. Disbursements.

1) Expenses paid in advance--

Commissioner v. Boylston Market Association, 131 F.2d 966 (1st Cir. 1942).

Facts. Boylston (P) is in the business of real estate management. P, a cash-basis taxpayer, purchased insurance policies that covered periods of three or more years. Rather than deduct the payments when made, P would prorate the expense over the term of years that each payment covered and allocate the cost accordingly. The Commissioner (D), stating that cash-basis taxpayers must deduct expenses when paid, assessed a deficiency. P paid and brought suit in the Tax Court, which held for P. D appeals.

Issue. Is a cash-basis taxpayer allowed to deduct for each tax year the pro rata portion of the prepaid insurance costs applicable to that year?

Held. Yes. Judgment affirmed.

♦ Prepaid insurance presents the same problems that arise in the acquisition of capital assets having a useful life of over one year. In such a case, the taxpayer can only take deductions for depreciation over the entire life of the asset. Prepaid insurance should be amortized over its life in the same manner that advance rentals and lease commissions are amortized.

Comment. Allowing a taxpayer to prorate life insurance payments over the period of coverage is a departure from strict cash-basis reporting. In Revenue Ruling 68-643, the IRS stated that it will determine the appropriateness of paying interest in advance on a case-by-case basis. The prepayment will be deductible when paid if no material distortion of income has resulted.

---

2) Mortgage points--

Cathcart v. Commissioner, 36 T.C.M. 1321 (1977).

Facts. In 1973, Cathcart (P) obtained a mortgage with a face amount of $57,600. Since this was a net proceeds mortgage, P received only $55,040. The difference was used to pay service charges and "points." P and the Commissioner (D) stipulate that the points are an additional interest charge. P deducted the full amount of the points, amounting to $1,087. D argues that the points should be amortized over the life of the mortgage.

Issue. Must points withheld from mortgage proceeds be amortized and deducted over the life of the loan?

Held. Yes. Judgment for D.

♦ Cash-basis taxpayers who prepay points on their home mortgages with funds not obtained from the lender are entitled to deduct the points in the year paid. However, if the points paid to obtain the loan are withheld from the loan proceeds rather than paid by the borrower, the related interest deduction must be amortized over the life of the loan.

Comment. If a taxpayer refinances a mortgage loan and uses part of the proceeds for improvements, the percentage of points prepaid in connection with the improvements can be deducted in the taxable year paid. [Revenue Ruling 87-22, 1987-1 Cum. Bull. 146]

3) **Checks.** A charitable contribution in the form of a check is deductible in the year the check is delivered, so long as the check is eventually honored and paid and there are no restrictions on the time and manner of payment. [Revenue Ruling 54-465, 1954-2 Cum. Bull. 93]

4) **Credit card transactions.** The Treasury has given qualified acceptance to the view that payment by credit card is the equivalent of borrowing cash from the credit card company and using it to pay the expense charged. Thus, if the expense charged is deductible, the taxpayer may take the deduction immediately.

5) **"Constructive payment"--**

Vander Poel, Francis & Co., Inc. v. Commissioner, 8 T.C. 407 (1947).

Facts. Vander Poel, Francis & Company is a cash-basis taxpayer. In 1942, the salaries of Vander Poel and Francis, two officers of the company, were paid by unconditional credits to their accounts. They each correctly reported the amounts as income constructively received for 1942, although neither actually withdrew the full amount during 1942. The company accordingly tried to deduct the entire salaries under the theory that if something was deemed received, it had to be deemed paid. The Commissioner disallowed the deduction, and this appeal followed.

Issue. Is there such a thing as the doctrine of "constructive payment" as a corollary to the doctrine of constructive receipt?

Held. No. Commissioner's determination sustained.

♦ The weight of authority is against the idea that "constructive payment" is a necessary corollary to the doctrine of constructive receipt. Although logic would seem to dictate that an item constructively received by a payee must have been constructively paid by the payor, deductions are a matter of legislative grace and are strictly delineated by statute. Unlike statutes designed to tax all income, deduction statutes must be fully met without the aid of assumption.

---

2. **Accrual Method.** This method of accounting recognizes items of income when they are *earned*, regardless of when they are received. Also, expense items are recognized when they are *incurred*, regardless of when they are actually paid. Problems of applying the accrual method usually arise in two contexts: (i) where it is uncertain whether an amount will be paid, and (ii) where an amount is received before it has been earned.

a. Income items.

1) General rule--

Spring City Foundry Co. v. Commissioner, 292 U.S. 182 (1934).

Facts. In 1920, Spring City Foundry Company (P), an accrual-basis taxpayer, sold goods on credit to a customer who later in the year declared bankruptcy. The Commissioner disallowed any bad-debt deduction for that year because there was not then any provision for a partially worthless debt in the I.R.C., and the debt had not yet become totally worthless. P then brought suit contending that it could reduce gross income for 1920 to reflect the loss.

Issue. May an accrual-basis taxpayer reduce gross income by the amount that a receivable has decreased in value during the year?

Held. No. Denial of reduction in income affirmed.

♦ Under the accrual method, income is based on the ***right*** to receive payment, not on the actual receipt of money. When the right to receive an amount becomes fixed, the right accrues. If, subsequently, the account receivable created by the credit sale becomes uncollectible, income is not reduced. The question rather becomes one of bad-debt deduction, which may or may not be allowed by the statute.

Comment. Gross income means the total sales, less the cost of goods sold, plus other income. Total sales must include the value of all completed sales for the year.

---

2) Judgments.
Under the accrual method of accounting, income is includible in gross income "when all events have occurred that fix the right to receive such income and the amount thereof can be determined with reasonable accuracy." [Revenue Ruling 70-151, 1970-1 Cum. Bull. 116] Thus in Revenue Ruling 70-151, the taxpayer had to include a judgment against the United States in the year the judgment became an acknowledged liability of the United States, rather than in the year Congress appropriated funds for payment.

3) Claim of right doctrine—income received subject to contingencies or liabilities--

---

North American Oil Consolidated v. Burnet, 286 U.S. 417 (1932).

Facts. North American Oil Consolidated (P) held certain oil properties that belonged to the United States. A suit was brought to oust P, and a receiver was appointed to manage the property and retain the income. The suit was settled in favor of P in 1917, and the receiver then turned over to the company the profits for 1916. The government appealed, and it was not until 1922 that the case was finally decided in favor of P. The Commissioner determined that the income should be included in the 1917 tax return. The Board of Tax Appeals found that it should be included in the 1916 return. The court of appeals overturned that decision, and the Supreme Court granted certiorari.

Issue. Should funds impounded by a receiver who is in control of only a portion of a corporation's property be taxed to the corporation when it finally has an unqualified right to receive them?

Held. Yes. Judgment affirmed.

♦ The receiver was not required to report the income in 1916 because he was the receiver of *only a part of the properties* operated by the company. The regulations contemplate a substitution of the receiver for the corporation, but this is realistic only if the receiver is in control of the *entire* corporation. Congress did not intend to have two separate returns filed (one by the receiver and one by the corporation).

♦ Whether the return for 1916 was filed on the cash basis or on the accrual basis, in neither event was the company taxable on income that it might never receive. There was no constructive receipt in 1916 because at no time could the company demand that the receiver pay over the money.

♦ The profits for 1916 became income to the company in 1917, when the company first became entitled to them and when it actually received them. If a taxpayer receives earnings under a claim of right and without restriction as to its disposition, he has received income that he is required to return, even though it may still be claimed that he is not entitled to the money, and even though he may still be adjudged liable to restore its equivalent.

Comment. The Court pointed out that if P had lost in 1922, it would have been able to take a deduction only from its profits of 1922.

————————————

4) **Unearned (prepaid or deferred) income.**

a) **Prepaid rent--**

New Capital Hotel, Inc. v. Commissioner, 28 T.C. 706 (1957).

Facts. New Capital Hotel, Inc., an accrual-basis taxpayer, leased hotel property it owned under a contract that provided for $30,000 per year rent, the last year's rent to be prepaid. The lease was to run from January 1, 1950, to December 31, 1959. When the lessee prepaid the $30,000 in 1949, New Capital reflected that transaction in an asset account titled "deposit on lease contract." The Commissioner assessed a deficiency of $11,724.50 for not reporting the prepaid rent as income in 1949. New Capital thereupon petitioned the Tax Court, arguing that the $30,000 prepayment should be included in income not in 1949, but in 1959, the year in which it would be earned.

Issue. Is prepaid income included in gross income in the year it is received?

Held. Yes. Decision for the Commissioner.

♦ The Commissioner is clearly within his discretion in determining that inclusion of prepaid income in the return for the year it was received is required to clearly reflect income. This is so even though it is not in accord with principles of commercial accounting.

♦ In this case, the money paid was clearly rent. Thus, this case is distinguishable from instances where money was paid as security to guarantee the performance of the lease's covenants and obligations.

---

b) Prepaid revenue--

Artnell Co. v. Commissioner, 400 F.2d 981 (7th Cir. 1968).

Facts. In early 1962, the Chicago White Sox, an accrual-basis taxpayer, was sold to Artnell Company (P). The return for the taxable year ending May 31, 1962, did not include in income proceeds from preseason sales of season tickets, single admissions, and parking books for games to be played after May 31. This amount was designated instead as deferred, unearned income on the balance sheet. The Commissioner (D) assessed a deficiency, and the Tax Court affirmed. P appeals on the ground that the law requires computation of taxable income under the accrual method of accounting regularly used by the taxpayer unless such method does not clearly reflect income. D asserts that any system that allows deferral of income "does not clearly reflect income."

Issue. Is it an abuse of discretion for D to disallow as not clearly reflective of income all systems of accounting that include deferral of income?

Held. Yes. Judgment reversed and case remanded.

♦ There must exist situations where the deferral of income will so clearly reflect income that the court will find an abuse of discretion if the Commissioner rejects it. Previous cases upholding the Commissioner did so on the basis that the time and extent of future services were uncertain. That uncertainty is not present in this case, where the income is allocable to games to be played in the future on a fixed schedule.

♦   However, the proof necessary to show that all relevant items were included in the calculation is missing. The case is reversed and remanded to determine whether the White Sox's method of accounting clearly reflected its income in its final taxable year.

Comments.

♦   On remand, P's accounting method was found to be proper.

♦   Under generally accepted accounting principles, income is not recognized until it is earned by delivery of the goods or services that the income is paying for. However, the IRS has taken the position that such amounts are income when they are received, independent of when delivery of the goods is made. But Revenue Procedure 71-21, 1971-2 C.B. 549, permits the taxpayer in certain instances to defer recognition of income until it is earned. The ruling applies only to a taxpayer who receives payment for future delivery of services. Deferment is allowed only if the services are to be rendered in full by the end of the tax year succeeding the tax year of prepayment. The ruling sets out guidelines and examples that illustrate the concept. While Supreme Court cases have held that prepaid income is taxable when received, *Artnell* held that a taxpayer will be permitted deferment if it can be shown that such would be the only proper way to account for the income.

———————

5)   **Inventories.** The formula for determining gross income is:

	Gross Sales
Less	Cost of Goods Sold
Equals	Gross Profit from Sales

The gross sales figure is simply total receipts from sales. It is more difficult, however, to determine the cost of the goods that were sold. In some cases it is possible to keep track of the cost of each specific item. For example, a car dealer has little difficulty in keeping track of the costs of each automobile sold. However, most manufacturers and retailers cannot possibly keep track of the cost of the numerous items they sell. This necessitates the use of inventories. The concept is quite simple:

	Opening Inventory
Plus	Purchases
Less	Closing Inventory
Equals	Cost of Goods Sold

The opening inventory is made up of all those goods on hand at the beginning of the year, and purchases are all the goods purchased during the year. The difficulty exists in valuing the units in the inventory at any given time. The cost of each batch of inventory purchases may vary from other batches bought at other times, and there is difficulty in determining which batch is sold at what time (and hence in valuing or determining the cost of the goods sold and the cost of the goods remaining in inventory). This is especially true in a consistently inflationary period (since the price of units purchased is constantly going up). Were the goods sold during the year on hand at the beginning of the year, or were they acquired at higher prices later in the year? In most cases, this question cannot be answered. In response to this problem, the IRS allows a taxpayer to compute her inventory by one of the following accepted methods.

a) **First in, first out.** If the first in, first out ("FIFO") method of inventory valuation is adopted, the taxpayer *assumes* that the goods first acquired were those that were first sold. The year-end inventory count is assumed to be made up of the goods last acquired. This method tends to show large profits in inflationary times, since the cost of goods sold (which is deducted from gross receipts to arrive at gross income) consists of the lower-priced goods first acquired.

b) **Last in, first out.** Under the last in, first out ("LIFO") method, the last goods acquired are assumed to have been sold first. The year-end inventory is assumed to be made up of items that were first acquired. In a period of rising prices, this means that the cost of goods sold is increased since the items sold were presumed to have been purchased later in the year. This in turn gives the taxpayer a larger deduction from gross receipts than the FIFO system, so that her gross income is smaller. I.R.C. section 472 authorizes the use of the LIFO method, with its reduction in reported taxable income. However, section 472(c) requires that if a taxpayer uses LIFO for tax purposes, she must also use it for reporting to creditors and shareholders. Many entities are more concerned with showing a strong financial picture than in the tax savings offered by use of LIFO and hence do not use the LIFO method.

b. **Deduction items.**

1) **Reserves.** Many taxpayers, faced with the refusal of courts to permit deferment of unearned income, have attempted to offset the immediate inclusion of prepaid income by immediately deducting the costs that would be incurred in the future in earning that income.

The accounting technique to accomplish this result is the use of "reserves" for estimated future expenses.

2) **Time for accrual of taxpayer's liability for interest.** Revenue Ruling 57-463 provides that a compromise agreement made subsequent to the year a taxpayer's liability for income tax deficiencies is determined, which merely fixes the rate and time of payment rather than the amount of tax liability, does not affect the time for accrual of the taxpayer's liability for interest.

3) **Future expense of carrying out a guarantee--**

Schuessler v. Commissioner, 230 F.2d 722 (5th Cir. 1956).

Facts. Schuessler (P), an accrual-basis taxpayer, sold 635 gas furnaces in 1946, each accompanied by a guarantee that it would be turned on and off each year for five years. Because this service would cost $2 per call, P set aside a reserve of $13,300 to cover the future service expenses. Each furnace had been sold for $20 to $25 more than those of the competition, which did not offer the guarantee. When P attempted to deduct this $13,300 in 1946, the Commissioner's (D's) disapproval was upheld in Tax Court. P appeals.

Issue. Can an accrual-basis taxpayer deduct the estimated future expense of carrying out a guarantee on goods sold in the business?

Held. Yes. Judgment reversed.

♦ The law contemplates an accounting method that accurately reflects the taxpayer's income on an annual accounting basis. An accounting system that accomplishes this objective is not subject to discretionary rejection by the Commissioner.

♦ P's plan not only does not offend any statutory requirement, but in fact is in accord with the language and intent of the law. While some other courts require strict mathematical certainty, this court will permit accrual of reasonably ascertainable future expenses necessary to earn or retain the income.

Comment. The Tax Reform Act of 1984 added I.R.C. section 461(h). This section requires that economic performance occur before a liability can be accrued. Economic performance includes rendering services, providing property, or payment. [I.R.C. §461(h)(2)] Consequently, the use of reserves is generally limited to bad debts.

---

3. **Other Methods.** Besides the cash method and the accrual method, the I.R.C. provides in section 453 for an installment method. In addition, many items

of income and expense are afforded special treatment throughout the I.R.C. Other accounting systems may be used if they conform with the following provision in the regulations: "Each taxpayer shall adopt such forms and systems as are, in his judgment, best suited to his need. However, no method of accounting is acceptable unless, in the opinion of the Commissioner, it clearly reflects income." [Treas. Reg. §1.446-1(a)(2)]

4. **Forced Matching of Methods.**

a. **Transaction between related parties.** I.R.C. section 267 disallows losses, expenses, and interest deductions between related parties. Under I.R.C. section 267, the related taxpayers are required to match the receipt of income and deduction of expenses. For example, an accrual-method taxpayer cannot deduct expenses accrued to a related cash-basis taxpayer.

b. **Multi-year lease agreements.** I.R.C. section 467 requires both the lessor and the lessee to use a consistent accrual method for the lease transaction.

C. TAXABLE YEAR

Income taxes are collected on a periodic basis. Therefore, the determination of net income must be based on an annual period. Even though a taxpayer is involved in transactions that stretch over several years, she must allocate income and deductions to each year and pay the applicable tax.

1. **Taxpayer's Restoration of Previously Taxed Income.**

a. **Mistaken claims--**

United States v. Lewis, 340 U.S. 590 (1951).

Facts. Lewis (P) received a bonus of $22,000, which he reported on his 1944 return. The bonus was erroneously calculated, and P's employer brought suit to recover half of it. In 1946, P lost the suit and repaid $11,000 to his employer. P sought to recompute his 1944 return to reflect an $11,000 bonus. The Commissioner (D) instructed P to claim a loss of $11,000 in 1946. The Court of Claims held that the excess bonus received under a mistake of fact was not income and held for P. The Supreme Court granted certiorari.

Issue. Are earnings that a taxpayer receives under a mistaken claim of right income?

Held. Yes. Judgment reversed.

♦ Nothing in the language of the claim of right rule permits an exception merely because a taxpayer is "mistaken" as to the validity of his claim. The claim of right doctrine has long been used to give finality to the annual accounting period and is now deeply rooted in the federal tax system.

Dissent (Douglas, J.). The taxpayer should be entitled to a refund of taxes paid in a prior tax year.

Comment. This case and others were materially affected by the passage of I.R.C. section 1341. This statute allows the taxpayer, if the amount exceeds $3,000, to claim the benefit of the deduction in either the earlier or later year, whichever would be more advantageous to him.

---

b. I.R.C. section 1341 and the claim of right doctrine--

Van Cleave v. United States, 718 F.2d 193 (6th Cir. 1983).

Facts. Van Cleave (P) was president and majority stockholder of Van-Mark Corporation. A corporate bylaw provided that if officers received compensation that the IRS (D) determined to be excessive, the officer must pay back the amount to the corporation. In 1974, P received $332,000 in salary and bonuses. In 1975, D determined that $57,500 of P's salary was excessive. In December 1975, P repaid the excessive amount to the corporation. P deducted the amount in 1975 and applied I.R.C. section 1341 to relate it back to the prior year. D allowed the 1975 deduction but refused to apply section 1341. The district court held that section 1341 was not available to P because his repayment was voluntary. P appeals.

Issue. If a restriction to a taxpayer's right to income does not arise until a year subsequent to the time of receipt, is section 1341 still applicable?

Held. Yes. Judgment reversed.

♦　　Even if a restriction on income does not arise until a year subsequent to its receipt, the section is still applicable. Therefore, the section 1341 tax adjustment is available in this situation if other requirements of the section are met.

Comment. Under the claim of right doctrine, if a taxpayer receives income under a claim of right and without restriction, he has received income even though it may be claimed that he is not entitled to retain the money and even though he may be liable to restore its equivalent. Section 1341 was enacted to alleviate the harsh effect of the claim of right doctrine. This case illustrates an instance where a taxpayer chose to deduct the amount of income repaid rather than claim a deduction in the later year of repayment.

---

2. Tax Benefit Doctrine--

Alice Phelan Sullivan Corp. v. United States, 381 F.2d 399 (Ct. Cl. 1967).

Facts. In 1939, Alice Phelan Sullivan Corporation (P) donated two parcels of land on the condition that they be used for charitable purposes. The property was returned in 1957, at which time P excluded it from income. The Commissioner (D), stating that the recovery was not a return of capital, made a deficiency assessment of $4,527.60 based on the 1957 tax rate of 52%. P paid the deficiency and brought suit in the Court of Claims.

Issue. Should the recovery of a prior year's deduction be taxed at the rates applicable to the year of deduction?

Held. No. D's motion for summary judgment granted.

♦ The recovery of property that was subject to a prior year's deduction must be treated as income in the year of recovery.

♦ To ensure the viability of the single-year concept, it is essential that annual income be ascertained without reference to previous losses or earlier tax rates.

♦ If no deduction was originally claimed or no tax savings resulted from the deduction, the "tax-benefit rule" would allow its exclusion from income when recovered in a subsequent year. In this case, P took a deduction in 1939, so the rule does not apply. Hence, the total recovery must be taxed as income using 1957 rates.

Comment. As long as the deduction brought a tax benefit, the amount of the tax savings is immaterial. However, had P not been able to benefit from the 1939 contribution (if, for example, P had no income in the year of the gift to offset against the deduction), the recovery of the property would not be taxable since there was no previous "benefit."

---

3. Income Averaging.

    a. Statutory income averaging. Prior to the Tax Reform Act of 1986, I.R.C. sections 1301 through 1304 provided a way for taxpayers with fluctuating yearly incomes to average out the high income so that it would be taxed as if received over four years. Beginning in 1987, the rules relating to income averaging were repealed.

    b. Do-it-yourself averaging. Taxpayers sometimes, through the use of contractual arrangements, trusts, or other devices, try to arrange that the income they earn in a given year will be spread over the next several years. For example, a professional football player has his bonus paid into an escrow to be distributed to him over a period of five years. In Revenue Ruling 60-31, 1960-1 C.B. 174, the IRS ruled on five different deferred compensation arrangements. The ruling held that income is taxable to the taxpayer in the year it is constructively received. Accordingly, careful planning may enable taxpayers to average income over a period of years.

c. **Statutory do-it-yourself averaging—deferred compensation plans.** Deferred compensation plans involve an employer providing compensation to an employee in years after the employee's services are performed. Unless the plan is carefully structured, the entire employee benefit will be taxed in the year earned (not when paid) under the constructive receipt doctrine or as an equivalent of cash. Before services are rendered, the employer and employee should settle the terms of the deferral. Congress has legislated certain types of plans that if followed will defer income to the employee until it is actually paid.

1) **Qualified pension plans.** If the employer complies with the guidelines of I.R.C. sections 401 through 415, contributions made to a pension or profit-sharing plan will be currently deductible to the employer but not taxed to the employee until she receives the payments after retirement. To qualify, the plan must be nondiscriminatory by including more than just company officers (*i.e.*, it must cover company employees as well). Also, the employer must comply with coverage, vesting, and funding requirements as set out by Congress.

2) **Self-employed persons.** Sole proprietors and partners can obtain the same favorable tax treatment given to the employees if they qualify under the above provisions.

3) **Employee contributions.** Employees generally can contribute up to $3,000 in an individual retirement account ("IRA") each year. However, individuals who are active participants in an employer plan and have adjusted gross income in excess of $54,000 on a joint return or $34,000 on a single return cannot deduct the IRA contribution.

4. **Carryover and Carryback Devices.**

a. **Net operating loss deduction.** The possibility that a taxpayer will be able to utilize the tax-benefit rule is greatly reduced by I.R.C. section 172. This provision permits a net operating loss to be carried back three years and then carried forward 15 years to offset the income in these years. Even though the loss will not bring a tax benefit in the year of loss, it will do so as it is carried back and forward.

b. **Net operating loss calculation.** If a taxpayer's business deductions (*e.g.,* interest, depreciation, bad debts, etc.) exceed her income, she has a net operating loss. Only expenditures attributable to a taxpayer's trade or business are included in this calculation. Personal deductions and investment deductions are not part of a net operating loss.

VI. THE CHARACTERIZATION OF INCOME AND DEDUCTIONS

A. CAPITAL GAINS AND LOSSES

1. Introduction.

Increases in the value of capital assets are as much a part of income in terms of accretion as wages, salaries, rents, interest, royalties, and other gains or receipts. In the past, capital gains (*e.g.,* gains from the sale of capital assets such as stocks, bonds, real property, etc.) were given preferential treatment. I.R.C. section 1202 allowed taxpayers a deduction of 60% of net long-term (held over six months) capital gains. However, capital losses were unfavorably treated. Capital losses were limited to offsetting capital gains plus $3,000 of ordinary income. In addition, net long-term capital losses were reduced by 50% when offsetting ordinary income.

The Tax Reform Act of 1986 repealed the I.R.C. section 1202 deduction and placed the ceiling rate on ordinary income and capital gains at 28%. The other capital gain sections were left unchanged. The Revenue Reconciliation Act of 1990 raised the upper rate on ordinary income to 31% and retained the 28% ceiling rate on capital gains. The current statute taxes most net capital gain at a 15% rate. A 5% capital gains rate applies to taxpayers in the 10% and 15% ordinary income tax brackets. Lower rates may apply to assets that have been held more than five years, but this only applies to appreciation accruing after January 1, 2001. Because of the benefit of lower tax rates for long-term capital gains, and the potential for negative limitations on the use of capital losses, it remains important to distinguish between ordinary and capital gains transactions. Listed below are some of the reasons that capital gains have been given favorable treatment.

a. **Bunching of income.** When they are taxed all at once, gains realized in one year that have accrued (been earned) over a period of years subject the taxpayer to unfairly high tax rates under the graduated income tax rate structure.

b. **Inflation.** In a period of inflation, capital gains are not real income to the extent that they merely reflect the rise in general prices.

c. **Lock-in effect.** Subjecting capital gains to a full tax induces investors to refrain from selling appreciated assets. This "lock-in" effect reduces liquidity and impairs the mobility of capital.

d. **Investment deterrent.** Taxation of capital gains tends to deter investors' willingness to bear the risks of investment. Without giving a tax benefit to the investor, society must pay the high price for high risk activities. This tends to slow the mobility of capital.

e. **Interest Rates.** When interest rates fluctuate, a portion of capital gain reflects a change in the rates at which income is capitalized, rather than reflecting true income.

2. **Mechanics of the Present Treatment of Capital Gains and Losses.** To determine the net capital gains and losses, the taxpayer must first determine whether she has "realized" gain or loss from the "sale or exchange" of a "capital asset." (The precise meaning of these terms is discussed below.) Then it must be determined whether the gain or loss realized must be "recognized." The gain or loss is then computed by subtracting the adjusted basis from the amount realized. The adjusted basis is the property's basis (acquisition cost) plus other capitalized expenditures (*i.e.*, amounts not deductible as current expenses), less depreciation and other receipts chargeable to the capital account. The amount realized from the sale of a capital asset is the sum of money received on sale plus the fair market value of property received (if any).

a. **Noncorporate taxpayers.** To arrive at the tax on capital transactions, the individual taxpayer follows these steps:

1) **Segregate long-term and short-term transactions.** Capital assets that a taxpayer sells or exchanges before she has held them for more than six months are treated differently than "long-term" capital assets (*i.e.,* those capital items held for more than six months).

2) **Net the amounts.** After the transactions are segregated by term, the short-term capital gains and losses are netted to reach a net short-term capital gain (or loss). The same is done with the long-term transactions to arrive at a net long-term capital gain or loss. The tax treatment depends on the amounts and classifications of the net long-term and net short-term amounts.

a) **Net short-term capital gain exceeds net long-term capital loss.** If this occurs, the excess short-term amount is treated as ordinary income.

b) **Net long-term capital gain exceeds net short-term capital loss.** The excess long-term capital gain is included in gross income. For example, suppose a taxpayer has taxable income of $15,000 and capital gains and losses as follows:

Long-term capital gain	—	$5,000
Long-term capital loss	—	$1,000
Short-term capital gain	—	$2,000
Short-term capital loss	—	$3,500

Netting the amounts would give the taxpayer a net long-term capital gain of $4,000 and a net short-term capital loss of

$1,500. The excess of net long-term capital gain is therefore $2,500. This total is added to ordinary income to arrive at a gross income of $17,500.

c) **Both short-term and long-term gains.** If both net amounts show gains, the combined amount is included in gross income.

d) **Net short-term capital loss exceeds net long-term capital gain.** I.R.C. section 1211 allows up to $3,000 of the excess net short-term capital loss to be deducted against ordinary income. The excess must be carried over to future years.

e) **Net long-term capital loss exceeds net short-term capital gain.** I.R.C. section 1211 allows up to $3,000 of the excess net long-term capital loss to be deducted against ordinary income. The excess must be carried over to future years.

f) **Both short-term and long-term losses.** If both netted amounts show losses, the short-term loss is used first against the $3,000 ceiling. Excess amounts are carried over to future years.

b. **Corporate taxpayers.** Corporations determine their net capital gains and losses the same way as noncorporate taxpayers.

1) **Net capital gains.** Under prior law, the excess of net long-term capital gains over net short-term capital losses was subject to an alternative tax of 28%. This aided only those corporations whose tax rate on ordinary income exceeded 28%. Since 1987, corporations have not received preferential treatment on capital gains.

2) **Net capital losses.** I.R.C. section 1211(a) allows corporations to deduct capital losses only to offset capital gains. The amount that is not used to offset capital gains may be carried back three years and forward five years and offset against those years' capital gains.

How Losses Are Utilized

	Individual	Corporation
Net operating loss	Carry back 3 years and forward 15 years *or* elect to carry forward 15 years only.	Same as individual.
Capital loss	Carry forward forever.	Carry back 3 years and forward 5 years.

3. The Meaning of "Capital Asset"

a. **Statutory definition.** Capital gains or losses are derived only from the sale or exchange of property constituting a "capital asset." Section 1221 of the I.R.C. includes all of a taxpayer's property as capital assets, *except:*

(i) Inventory;

(ii) Accounts receivable and notes receivable;

(iii) Assets used in a trade or business (but not I.R.C. section 1231 assets);

(iv) Artistic, musical, or literary compositions if held by the creator or someone who received them from the creator by gift or inheritance, or letters or memoranda if held by the person who wrote them or the person to whom they were sent;

(v) Certain kinds of stock options; and

(vi) Certain government bonds.

Everything else is a capital asset. The courts have construed the exceptions broadly in denying favorable capital gains treatment. However, taxpayers have used these cases as precedent in avoiding unfavorable capital loss treatment.

1) **Property held for sale to customers.** I.R.C. section 1221(1) excludes from capital asset treatment property "held by the taxpayer primarily for sale to customers in the ordinary course of his trade or business." Any gain or loss on the sale of such property is ordinary income.

a) **Factors in characterization of assets--**

Mauldin v. Commissioner, 195 F.2d 714 (10th Cir. 1952).

Facts. In 1921, Mauldin (P) acquired title to 160 acres of land one-half mile outside Clovis, New Mexico. He intended to use it to operate a cattle business, but because of drought, crop failures, and bank failures, along with a drop in the cattle business, he abandoned that plan. When he was unsuccessful at selling the entire tract at a loss, he divided it into small tracts and blocks and built a home in the middle. However, no lots were sold until 1931, when the land began to be included in the city limits. In 1939, the city assessed P $25,000 for a paving project. In order to pay the liens, P carried on an aggressive sales campaign in 1939 and 1940. After that, P devoted his time to a lumber business and decided to hold the land for investment. Due to great demand for the lots, varying numbers of lots were sold between 1941 and 1948. On his tax return for 1944, P did not designate the nature of his business, but in 1945, it was listed as "lumber and real estate." On both returns, he showed the lots sold as long-term capital assets and computed the tax accordingly. The Commissioner (D) determined the profit to be ordinary income and assessed additional tax. The Tax Court sustained D, and P appeals on the ground that after 1940, his business status was changed and he held the lots only for investment purposes, not for sale to customers in the ordinary course of trade or business.

Issue. When sales are continuous and frequent, is that sufficient to show that the character of an asset has changed?

Held. Yes. Judgment affirmed.

◆   The primary purpose or use of an asset, which determines its nature, can change during its life. Although there is no fixed formula, a number of factors are helpful in determining when the change occurred, such as whether the property was acquired for sale or investment, and continuity and frequency of sales.

◆   When P subdivided the land and offered it for sale, it changed from investment property to land held for sale in the ordinary course of trade or business. P argued that after 1940, it changed back to investment property. However, the record shows that in 1945, he sold even more lots on a seller's market, without solicitation, than he had sold in 1940 in a buyer's market. In addition, although he was in the lumber business, a substantial part of his income came from the sale of these lots. Hence, the findings of the Tax Court cannot be overturned.

---

b)   **Interpretation of "primarily"--**

Malat v. Riddell, 383 U.S. 569 (1966).

Facts. Malat (P) and others purchased a 45-acre parcel of land. P stated that they intended to build and run an apartment complex on the land. When P could not obtain financing, he and his partners subdivided and sold portions of the parcel and recognized ordinary income thereon. After other difficulties were encountered, P sold his interest in the venture and claimed a capital gain on the sale. The Commissioner (D) assessed P with a tax deficiency, stating that P had a dual purpose in purchasing the land, which would place the land within the I.R.C. section 1221(1) exception and preclude capital gain treatment.

Issue. Is "primarily" as used in section 1221(1) meant to mean a "substantial" purpose?

Held. No. Judgment vacated and case remanded.

♦ "Primarily" means of first importance or principally. P's primary purpose in acquiring the land was to construct an apartment complex. When this goal became unattainable, P was forced to sell his interest in the land. This sale was not the primary purpose behind P's purchase and therefore should be given capital gains treatment.

Comment. The Supreme Court did not make the determination that the land was a capital asset. The district court came to this conclusion on remand.

---

4. **The Sale or Exchange Requirement.** For a transaction to be taxed as a capital gain or loss, the provisions of I.R.C. sections 1222 and 1231 require that a sale or exchange occur. At times the courts have confused the "sale or exchange" requirement with the previously discussed "capital asset" requirement. The distinction between the two is not a clear one. In other contexts, the courts have ignored the "sale or exchange" requirement, as was done in *Arrowsmith, infra,* where the payment of a judgment was characterized as a capital loss. The courts have usually focused more attention on the status of the asset than on the manner of its disposition.

a. **Satisfaction of a claim: the debtor's situation--**

Kenan v. Commissioner, 114 F.2d 217 (2d Cir. 1940).

Facts. Bingham died in 1917. In her will, she placed her residuary estate in a trust. The trustees (Ps) were to pay Bingham's niece a certain amount until the niece reached 40, at which time Ps were directed to pay the niece $5 million in cash or securities. When such time came, Ps paid the niece partly in stock and partly in cash. The Commissioner (D) determined that the distribution of the securities to the niece was a "sale or exchange" to Ps and thus resulted in capital gains taxable to Ps. Ps contend that the delivery of securities to the legatee was a nontaxable donative disposition.

Issue. Does payment under set trust terms constitute a sale or exchange?

Held. Yes. Judgment affirmed.

♦ The legatee had a claim against the estate for $5 million, payable in either cash or securities. She took none of the chances of a residuary legatee, whose claim would consist of a share of securities that could decline in value. Her claim was of a set value payable at a certain time.

♦ The fact that the disposition was effectuated by a will does not disqualify it as not being a "sale or exchange." "Exchange" does not necessarily have the connotation of a binding oral agreement (which may attach to the word "sale").

Comment. The party transferring property in satisfaction of a claim is participating in a sale or exchange and hence receives capital gain treatment. However, the party whose claim is satisfied (the legatee in this case) is not so regarded since payment is not an exchange. Compare this with the next case.

---

   b.   **Satisfaction of a claim--**

Hudson v. Commissioner, 20 T.C. 734 (1953).

Facts. Harahan obtained a judgment for $75,702.12 against Cole on November 23, 1929. Harahan later died, and Taylor and Hudson purchased the judgment from her residuary legatees in 1943. In May 1945, Cole paid Taylor and Hudson $21,150 as full settlement of the judgment against him. Taylor and Hudson had incurred $11,004 of expenses in collecting the judgment. Accordingly, Hudson realized a $5,073 gain, which he treated as a capital gain by reporting half of it ($2,536.50) on his 1945 tax return. The Commissioner determined the gain to be ordinary income, and Hudson petitioned the court for a determination.

Issue. Is capital gain realized on a settlement between the judgment debtor and the assignee or transferee of a prior judgment creditor?

Held. No. Decision for Commissioner.

◆   The result of this kind of transaction is that a debt is paid or extinguished. There can be no sale or exchange of property because there is no property in existence after the transaction. Thus, even though a judgment is a capital asset, there is no sale or exchange of capital assets within the meaning of the statute, and hence no capital gain.

---

   c.   **Sale or license.** When a franchise, trademark, or trade name is transferred, the question often arises whether the transfer should be treated as a sale (and accorded capital gains treatment) or a license (with the proceeds looked on as ordinary income). Generally, capital gains treatment is allowed only if the transferor did not reserve any significant powers, rights, or continuing interests with respect to the subject matter of the franchise, trademark, or trade name. In the usual franchise, the franchisor retains strict controls over the franchisee's operation. Payments received by the franchisor are ordinary income.

   5.   **Holding Period**. To qualify as a long-term capital gain or loss, the taxpayer must hold the asset over one year. If the asset is held one year or less, its sale

or exchange gives rise to a short-term capital gain or loss. The holding period is measured from the time the asset was acquired to the time it was disposed of. The holding period begins to run on the day following the date of acquisition of the asset involved. [Revenue Ruling 66-7, 1966-1 Cum. Bull. 188] The holding period for debentures, stocks, and securities acquired by purchase is determined by excluding the "trade date" (*i.e.*, the date on which the contract to buy or sell is made) on which they are acquired and including the trade date on which they are sold. [Revenue Ruling 66-97, 1966-1 Cum. Bull. 190] Note that a new holding period begins only if the property's basis changed when the taxpayer acquired the property. If the acquired capital asset retains its previous owner's basis, then the acquiring taxpayer adds or "tacks" the previous owner's holding period to his own. For example, if A acquires a capital asset by gift, her basis is the "substituted basis" of the donor. A is entitled to tack the donor's holding period to her own in determining whether her gain or loss upon disposal is long term.

6. **Judicial View.**

   a. **"Income" property.**

      1) **Cancellation of a lease--**

Hort v. Commissioner, 313 U.S. 28 (1941).

Facts. Hort (P) inherited a building subject to a long-term lease. One of P's tenants wished to terminate the lease prior to its expiration date. P settled the lease for $140,000 and claimed a deduction for the difference between the rental value of the unexpired lease term and the $140,000 actually received. The Commissioner (D) disallowed this "loss" and included the entire amount of the $140,000 in gross income. P filed suit for a refund, and the Tax Court and the circuit court both affirmed the Commissioner's ruling. P appeals.

Issue. When a lessor receives cash compensation prior to the expiration of the lease term, and the amount received is less than the full rental payments that would have been received on the lease had it not been terminated, is the full amount received immediately recognizable as ordinary income?

Held. Yes. Judgment affirmed.

♦   P received an amount of money in lieu of the future rental income he was entitled to under the lease. That rental income would have been ordinary income.

♦   The fact that P received less than he would have under the lease does not entitle him to a deduction for the difference.

♦   The consideration received was not a return of capital. A lease is a capital asset. However, the payments were a substitute for rental payments, not for the sale or exchange of the lease. Therefore, the gain recognized is ordinary income, not a return of capital.

---

2)   Sale of a leasehold interest--

Metropolitan Building Co. v. Commissioner, 282 F.2d 592 (9th Cir. 1960).

Facts. On December 3, 1907, Metropolitan Building Company (P) acquired a lease executed by the University of Washington on four square blocks in downtown Seattle. On August 1, 1922, P sublet most of one block for the construction of the Olympic Hotel. In 1936, Olympic, Inc., acquired the sublease, which was due to terminate on October 31, 1954, one day before the master lease. In 1952, the University of Washington started trying to set up a long-term arrangement for the lease of the hotel following the expiration of P's release of rights under the master lease. An arrangement was subsequently reached whereby Olympic, Inc., paid $137,000 to P to convey, quitclaim, assign, and release to the state of Washington all of its right, title, and interest in and to that portion of the leasehold on which the Olympic Hotel was located. The university then immediately leased to Olympic. The Commissioner (D) contended that the entire $137,000, including money for P's just share of the ad valorem personal property tax assessed against the leasehold and the money for increased taxes, was ordinary income. The Tax Court upheld the Commissioner, and P appeals.

Issue. Is the sale of a leasehold interest the transfer of a capital asset?

Held. Yes. Judgment reversed.

♦   The money was paid to P not merely to discharge Olympic's obligation to pay rent. It was paid for the purchase of P's entire leasehold interest. In other words, the transaction was not a liquidation of a right to future income, but a sale of the income-producing property itself. As a capital asset, the leasehold interest held value beyond the fixed rental payments due, and any gain realized through its sale was therefore capital gain under the I.R.C.

♦   D conceded that if the consideration had been paid by the university or if the lease had been assigned to a third party, the transaction would have constituted a sale. However, the nature of the transaction is not controlled by the person of the payor.

Comment. Other cases have recognized as a capital asset such things as an income interest in a trust.

---

b. **Effect of prior transactions.** In a number of cases, transactions have been classified as capital or ordinary because they were related to previous transactions.

   1) **Lookback rule--**

Arrowsmith v. Commissioner, 344 U.S. 6 (1952).

Facts. In 1937, Arrowsmith (P) and the other shareholders decided to liquidate their corporation. Distributions were made in the following four years. P reported the profits as capital gains. In 1944, after the final liquidation, a judgment, which the two previous shareholders were required to pay, was rendered against the old corporation. P deducted his payment as an ordinary loss. The Commissioner (D) viewed the payment as part of the original liquidation, which would require capital loss treatment. The Tax Court held for P, but the court of appeals reversed. The Supreme Court granted certiorari.

Issue. May transactions of separate tax years be integrated for purposes of classifying one of them as capital or ordinary?

Held. Yes. Judgment affirmed.

♦   Examining related transactions to classify one of them is not an attempt to reopen or readjust a previous tax year. It is apparent that P should not be allowed to receive favorable capital gain treatment on the original distribution and then claim ordinary loss treatment on payment of the judgment.

Dissent (Douglas, J.). Each year is a separate unit for tax accounting purposes. We impeach that principle when we treat this year's losses as if they diminished last year's gains.

Dissent (Jackson, Frankfurter, JJ.). Congress has not authorized the reopening of previous tax years for these purposes. Also, had the liability been paid by the corporation before liquidation, it would have deducted the payment as an ordinary loss.

   2) **Limitations imposed on the refund--**

United States v. Skelly Oil Co., 394 U.S. 678 (1969).

Facts. Because of a court ruling, Skelly Oil Company (P) was required to refund $505,537 in 1958 to two customers. This amount had been paid to P and included in its gross income for the years 1952 through 1957. Because of a depletion allowance of 27.5%, only $366,514 was included in P's gross income during those years. In claiming a refund, P attempted to deduct the full $505,537. The Commissioner (D) disallowed the claim and assessed a deficiency. P paid and filed suit in district court, which held for D. The court of appeals reversed, and D appeals.

Issue. Is a deduction under claim of right limited to the amount that was previously taxed?

Held. Yes. Judgment reversed.

- Nothing in I.R.C. section 1341 implies that a deduction must equal the item that was included in gross income. Congress did not intend to give a deduction for refunding money that was not taxed when received.

- The annual accounting period normally requires that the tax consequences of the receipt should not determine the size of the deduction allowable in the year of repayment. Nevertheless, this does not require us to close our eyes to what happened in prior years.

7. **Statutorily Created Capital Gain and Loss Consequences.**

   a. **Business or nonbusiness property?--**

Stephen P. Wasnok v. Commissioner, 30 T.C.M. 39 (1971).

Facts. In 1960, Stephen and Mary Wasnok bought a house in Cincinnati. Spring Grove Loan Company loaned the money and held a first mortgage on the property. When Stephen and Mary moved to California in 1961, they were unable to sell the house. During the next four years, they rented it out for an average of $200 per month. Although it was listed twice, no buyer offered a satisfactory price. Finally, in May 1965, Stephen and Mary, threatened with foreclosure, deeded the property back to the mortgage company. They had taken depreciation deductions from 1961 to 1964 totaling $4,697.42, and thus the difference between the adjusted basis and the mortgage balance produced a loss of $3,611.24. No returns were filed for 1965 and 1966 because there did not appear to be any tax due. Stephen and Mary took capital loss carryforward deductions of $1,000 on their 1967 separate returns and $389 on their 1968 joint return. The Commissioner disallowed the carryforward capital loss deductions on the ground that the loss was ordinary, and could be deducted only in the year of the loss (1965). The Wasnoks therefore brought this action.

Issue. Does nonbusiness property become property used in a trade or business when the owners, for lack of a buyer, are forced to rent it for a fairly continuous period, and claim deductions for expenses and depreciation on their tax return?

Held. Yes. Commissioner's determination affirmed.

♦ Nonbusiness property can be changed by subsequent use in a trade or business. In this case, more or less continuous rental, combined with deductions for depreciation and expenses, establishes the use of the property in a rental business. Hence, under I.R.C. section 1231, which makes depreciable property and real property (depreciable or not) used in a trade or business a noncapital asset, the loss was one on a noncapital asset. Thus, the loss was ordinary and should have been taken in 1965.

---

b. Sale of a going business--

Williams v. McGowan, 152 F.2d 570 (2d Cir. 1945).

Facts. Williams (P) had a hardware business with a partner. When the partner died, P purchased the partner's interest from the estate and then sold the entire business interest to a third party. He suffered a loss on the transaction, which he reported as an ordinary loss on his tax return. The Commissioner (D) determined that the sale of the business qualified as a capital transaction and assessed P with a tax deficiency. P paid and brought suit in district court, which held for D. P appeals.

Issue. Does the sale of a sole proprietorship result in capital gain or loss?

Held. No. Judgment reversed.

♦ While the sale of a partner's interest is treated as a capital transaction, this business became a sole proprietorship when P bought his partner's interest. No special treatment is accorded to the sale of a sole proprietorship. In defining "capital assets," Congress plainly desired that the sole proprietorship be looked on as a group of individual assets.

♦ In this case, the depreciable fixtures and inventory both fall within exceptions to the capital asset definition. No other sold asset gives rise to capital gain, except possibly the receivables. The case is therefore remanded to determine the nature of the receivables. The remainder of the items are not capital assets.

Dissent. Congress did not intend to carve the sale of a business into separate distinct sales. The parties contracted for the transfer of an entire business. It should be a capital gain or loss.

Comment. This case illustrates the "fragmentation theory," which is used when an unincorporated proprietorship is sold. The sale of an incorporated business gives rise to capital gain unless the corporation is collapsible under I.R.C. section 341.

B. CHARACTERIZATION ON THE SALE OF DEPRECIABLE PROPERTY

I.R.C. section 1221(2) excludes from the capital asset category "property, used in [a taxpayer's] trade or business, of a character which is subject to the allowance for depreciation provided in section 167, or real property used in his trade or business." However, I.R.C. section 1231 provides that even though this property is not a "capital asset," gain realized on the disposition of "property used in a trade or business" will be treated as if it were a capital asset.

1. **I.R.C. Section 1231 Formula.**

    a. **Firepot calculation.** The first level of calculations to determine section 1231 gain or loss is the involuntary conversion, or "firepot," calculation. If losses from theft, fire, storm, or other casualties exceed gains, they are ordinary losses. If gains exceed losses, their total is brought forth to the second calculation, referred to as the "hotchpot."

    b. **Hotchpot calculation.** The hotchpot begins with the gains and losses brought from the firepot calculation. Added to this amount are condemnations of capital assets held over one year, or property used in a trade or business. Finally, gains and losses from sales or exchanges of business property are added in. If the net amount is a loss, it is ordinary. However, if the net amount is a gain, it is characterized as a long-term capital gain.

2. **I.R.C. Section 1231 Assets.** Section 1231 is a means of allowing capital gain treatment for noninventory business investment assets. Remember that the capital gains provisions were designed to apply to gains and losses on the disposition of long-term investment property, rather than dispositions resulting from the day-to-day operation of a business. Section 1231 was enacted for the taxpayer who uses long-term "investment" property in his business. To qualify for section 1231, property must be more akin to long-term investment property than to short-term use as inventory or business property. In addition to this "investment" test, property must also not fall under other exclusions. Depreciable personal property will not qualify if it is held "primarily for sale to customers in the ordinary course of business." The same exclusion applies to real property. If such property is inventory to the taxpayer or held for sale, it will not qualify under section 1231's nebulous requirements. The result is that the determination of what is a section 1231 asset has been left largely to judicial interpretation.

3. **Characterization Under I.R.C. Section 1239--**

United States v. Parker, 376 F.2d 402 (5th Cir. 1967).

Facts. In 1959, Parker (P) and his long-time employee, Eaves, incorporated Parker's retail oil and gasoline business. Parker took 800 shares in exchange for $93,400 worth of property, and Eaves subscribed to the remaining 200 shares, paying $7,500 down and $23,350 over five years. The corporation had right of first refusal. An agreement between the stockholders provided that when Eaves terminated his employment, Parker would buy his shares at fair market value, excluding goodwill. This restriction was noted on Eaves's shares only. At the first meeting of the board of directors, Parker sold over $95,000 worth of depreciable property to the corporation. He reported the gain as long-term capital gain. The Commissioner (D) characterized the gain as ordinary income and assessed a deficiency on the grounds that Parker owned more than 80% in value of the corporation. P paid and sued for a refund in district court. The Commissioner appeals the granting of a motion for summary judgment.

Issue. If one corporate share is subject to a restriction of an important nature that does not bind another share of stock, is the second share inherently worth more as a matter of law?

Held. Yes. Judgment for Commissioner.

♦ Any significant restriction on one share of stock that is not on a second makes the second inherently worth more as a matter of law. In this case, the fact that Parker had effective control of the corporation's affairs, along with the restrictions noted on Eaves's shares, made Parker's shares inherently more valuable.

♦ I.R.C. section 1239 prevents capital gain treatment of a sale or exchange of depreciable property to a controlled corporation or a spouse. Control is defined as "more than 80% in value." Parker owned exactly 80% of the shares, but since his shares were worth more than Eaves's, he owned more than 80% in value of the corporation. Therefore, the sale was to a controlled corporation and resulted in ordinary gain.

Comment. The test is now "80% or more." Note also that any loss under section 1239 is not deductible at all.

---

4. **Recapture of Depreciation.** Much of the property eligible for I.R.C. section 1231 treatment is also property that can be depreciated under section 167. Thus, a taxpayer could take ordinary depreciation deductions and then claim a capital gain upon disposition of the property. Sections 1245 and 1250 were enacted to eliminate this taxpayer practice, which had the effect of converting ordinary income into capital gain. These sections require a taxpayer to report certain portions of section 1231 gain as ordinary income.

a. **Tangible depreciable personal property.** I.R.C. section 1245 applies to *tangible depreciable personal property*. Upon the sale of tangible depreciable personal property, any gain realized is ordinary income to the extent of all depreciation deductions taken after 1961. In other words, all depreciation taken since 1961 must be recaptured on a sale of a section 1245 asset. For example, suppose a taxpayer bought a machine in 1990 for $20,000 and deducted $12,000 depreciation from 1990 to 1999. If in 1999, he sells the machine for $23,000, the gain realized is $15,000. Section 1245 requires that $12,000 of this gain be recognized as ordinary income. The remaining $3,000 receives capital gain treatment.

1) **Conversion of section 1245 property to personal use.** Revenue Rule 69-487 provides that the conversion of section 1245 property to personal use is not a disposition of the property; thus, there is no gain to be recognized by the taxpayer upon the conversion. However, the provisions of section 1245 will apply to any disposition of the property by the taxpayer at a later date.

b. **Depreciable real property.** I.R.C. section 1250 applies to depreciable real property that is not section 1245 property. It requires that "excess" depreciation claimed on buildings be recaptured. This means any depreciation in excess of the straight-line rate. For example, suppose that a taxpayer purchased a commercial building in 1990 for $100,000. The building had an expected useful life of 50 years. When the building was sold in 2000, depreciation of $32,000 had been claimed. Of this, the straight-line amount was $20,000. If the building had been sold for $85,000, the gain realized would be $17,000 since the basis at that date was $68,000. Section 1250 requires that $12,000 of the $17,000 gain be recognized as ordinary income, since that amount represents accelerated depreciation over the straight-line rate.

1) **Exception.** Under I.R.C. section 1250(a)(1)(B), a special recapture rule applies for owners of housing units for low-income renters. In such cases, there is full recapture only if the property is held less than 100 months. Thereafter, the amount recaptured is reduced by 1% for each month held over 100 months. There is no recapture if the property is held for 200 months.

C. DEDUCTIONS AFFECTED BY CHARACTERIZATION PRINCIPLES

1. **Bad Debts and Worthless Securities.** A bad debt is an obligation owed to the taxpayer that becomes uncollectible. For the taxpayer to be able to claim a deduction, the loss must arise from a valid debt arising from a true debtor-creditor relationship. The taxpayer must show that no hope of repayment exists (*i.e.,* that the receivable has become worthless).

a. **True debtor-creditor relationship--**

Howard S. Bugbee v. Commissioner, 34 T.C.M. 291 (1975).

Facts. Howard S. Bugbee was president of Poop Deck, Inc., a corporation that operated a beer parlor in Hermosa Beach, California. In 1957, he became acquainted with a customer, Paul Billings. Their friendship grew, and Billings was even named godfather to one of the Bugbee children. Bugbee was impressed with some of the business ventures Billings had in mind. As a result, he made loans of over $19,750 to Billings between September 1958 and December 1960 for use in those business ventures. The obligations were evidenced by 11 unsecured, unconditional demand notes providing for 6% interest. Bugbee never investigated Billings's financial position but asserts that he intended to be repaid after one of the business ventures succeeded. However, repayment was not conditioned on the success of any of these ventures. (For his part, Billings still acknowledges these debts and at trial asserted his intention to repay the notes if possible.) In 1966, Bugbee deducted the $19,750 as a personal bad debt and took a short-term capital loss. The Commissioner disallowed the loss on the ground that a debtor-creditor relationship did not exist. Bugbee petitioned the court.

Issue. Does a debtor-creditor relationship exist if, at the time of transfer, both parties intended to establish an enforceable obligation of repayment?

Held. Yes. Commissioner's determination reversed.

- ♦ The Commissioner argued that the debts were worthless when the money was advanced because they did not give rise to a reasonable expectation of repayment. However, the key is the genuineness of repayment prospects in light of economic realities and the parties' intent. Bugbee believed that Billings would probably be able to pay after he engaged in a successful business venture. As long as repayment was not intended to be conditioned on such success but was intended by Bugbee and Billings to be unconditional and enforceable, a debtor-creditor relationship arose.

- ♦ The evidence indicates that the loans were not investments in Billings's enterprises. Bugbee was not entitled to share in any of the profits.

- ♦ Although Bugbee and Billings were close personal friends, they were not related and their relationship did not have a long history. In addition, Bugbee did not have the financial resources to advance the funds without expectation of repayment. Thus, the loans were not a gift.

---

   b. **Business and nonbusiness bad debts.** Business bad debts are wholly deductible from the taxpayer's income. Nonbusiness bad debts receive less favorable short-term capital loss treatment.

1) **Investment loans.** Loans to parties with whom the taxpayer has invested money are given nonbusiness status, since an investment does not qualify as a trade or business.

2) **Family loans.** Bona fide loans to family members are nonbusiness loans.

3) **Shareholder's loans to a corporation--**

Charles J. Haslam v. Commissioner, 33 T.C.M. 482 (1974).

Facts. In 1954, Haslam and Canavan established Northern Explosives, Inc. ("Northern"). Each received 50% of the stock for a $10,000 investment. Haslam managed the business and was also employed by the corporation as a salesman at a salary of $15,000 per year plus fringe benefits. Canavan took no active part in the business. In 1957, Haslam bought Canavan's interest for $10,000. In 1960, Northern had financial difficulties and was forced to borrow $100,000, which Haslam guaranteed personally by pledging his home and some marketable securities. In 1961, the corporation went into Chapter 11 status, and in 1964, it went bankrupt. Haslam's securities were sold, and $55,956 was applied toward the debt. In 1967, Haslam claimed a business bad debt of $55,956 on the guarantee of Northern's loans. The Commissioner disallowed the deduction on the ground that it was a nonbusiness bad-debt deductible as a short-term capital loss only. Haslam petitioned the court.

Issue. If the dominant motive for guaranteeing a loan to a corporation in which one is both an employee and shareholder is to protect one's employment position (rather than one's investment), is a loss occasioned thereby a business bad-debt loss?

Held. Yes. Decision for Haslam.

♦ Under I.R.C. section 166, business bad-debt losses are deductible against ordinary income, while nonbusiness bad-debt losses are deductible only as short-term capital losses (with the attendant $3,000 restriction). A debt will qualify as a business bad debt if it bears a direct relationship to the taxpayer's trade or business. In this case, there was a direct relationship to Haslam's trade or business as an employee, since the guarantee was required to keep the corporation in business.

♦ However, being an investor in a corporation is not a trade or business. Thus, where a taxpayer sustains a loss on a guarantee to a corporation in which he has both an employee and a stockholder interest, a proximate relationship between the taxpayer's trade or business as an employee and his loss is established only if the taxpayer's dominant motivation in entering in the guarantee was to protect employee interest (rather than the investor interest). The facts of this case indicate that Haslam had no other employment and that his particular expertise in explosives was not readily marketable. He testified that he guaranteed the loans primarily to protect his job. Certainly an assured salary of $15,000 per year was more valuable than protecting a $20,000 investment. Thus, Haslam's dominant motivation was to protect his interest as an employee, and the business bad-debt deduction should have been allowed.

---

c. **Reserve for bad debts.** A taxpayer may take a bad-debt deduction before the debt actually becomes uncollectible if a reserve account is set up and a reasonable prediction is made by the taxpayer.

d. **Recovery of bad debts.** Bad debts taken as a deduction but subsequently recovered must be included in gross income in the year received. However, if all or any portion of the prior bad-debt deduction did not result in a tax benefit to the taxpayer (*i.e.,* did not result in a reduction of his taxes), then he may exclude a portion of the recovery to the extent the previous bad-debt deduction failed to effect a tax benefit.

2. **Charitable Contributions.** Taxpayers are entitled to a deduction for contributions to recognized charities—basically, to the government or any entity organized and operated predominantly for charitable, religious, scientific, literary, or educational purposes.

   a. **Limitations as to amount.**

      1) **Individual taxpayers.** Individuals are allowed to deduct up to *50% of their adjusted gross income* for gifts to most charities. (Gifts to "nonoperating" private foundations are limited to 20%.) Excess contributions can be carried forward for five years.

      2) **Corporations.** Corporations can deduct gifts only up to *5% of net income*. Excess contributions can be carried forward five years.

      3) **Estates and trusts.** Estates and trusts have *no limit* on the amount of charitable contributions deductible.

   b. **Contributions for valuable consideration.** Taxpayers cannot deduct payments to charity for which they obtain economic benefits.

      1) **Contributions to private schools.** Revenue Ruling 83-104, 1983-2 C.B. 46, analyzes situations whereby parents of students "contribute" to the private school. The ruling holds that no deduction is allowed in situations where the "contribution" is really a payment of tuition.

      2) **Fund raising activities.** Revenue Ruling 67-246, 1967-2 C.B. 104, provides that amounts paid for admission and purchasing items are not deductible. However, if taxpayers pay more than fair market value for an item, the excess is a contribution.

c.   **Gifts of appreciated property.**

1)   **Prior law.** Before the Tax Reform Act of 1969, a taxpayer could deduct the fair market value of property donated to charity. This gave the taxpayer the advantage of deducting the full value of the property without having to recognize a gain for the appreciation.

2)   **Present law.** The taxpayer may still deduct the fair market value of donated property if that property would, if sold, produce long-term capital gain. This deduction is limited to 30% of the donor's adjusted gross income.

a)   **Exceptions.** If the gift is to a private foundation or is of tangible personal property unrelated to the charity's function, the amount of the deduction is reduced by 50% of the gain that would have been recognized had the property been sold.

b)   **Short-term capital gain property.** The taxpayer who donates short-term capital gain or ordinary income property may claim only a charitable deduction not to exceed his basis in the property. This deduction is reduced further by any depreciation that would have been recaptured had the property been sold.

d.   **Bargain sales.** If a taxpayer sells property to a charity for a price below fair market value, the difference (the bargain element) is deductible as a charitable contribution.

1)   The transaction is treated as part sale and part gift, and the bargain seller is required to apportion his basis, which means that there will be a partial realization of gain.

2)   For example, if T sells shares of stock (held for more than one year) to a public charity at his cost, $12,000, although the stock is presently worth $20,000, T is entitled to an $8,000 charitable contribution deduction. But his basis in the stock at time of sale is deemed to be only 12/20 of cost—*i.e.,* $7,200 instead of $12,000—so that T realizes a $4,800 gain.

e.   **Donated services and free use of property.** The value of personal services donated to a charity is not deductible. Also, if a taxpayer allows a charity to use his property rent-free, he may not deduct the value of the forgone rent as a charitable deduction. However, a taxpayer's out-of-pocket expenses in aiding a charity are deductible.

3.   **Casualty and Theft Losses.**

a.   **Nature of losses allowed.** I.R.C. section 165(c)(3) allows deductions for personal losses arising from "fire, storm, shipwreck, or other casualty or from theft." A "casualty" has been defined as "an accident, a mishap, some sudden invasion by a hostile agency; it excludes the progressive deterioration of property through a steadily operating cause." [Fay v. Helvering, 120 F.2d 253 (2d Cir. 1941)]

1) **Termite damage.** Revenue Ruling 63-232 states that termite damage to nonbusiness property is not deductible as a casualty loss under section 165(c)(3).

2) **Decline in value--**

Pulvers v. Commissioner, 407 F.2d 838 (9th Cir. 1969).

Facts. A landslide demolished three homes in the Pulvers' (Ps') neighborhood. The fear of future landslides caused a reduction in the value of their property. They deducted this as an "other casualty loss" on their income tax return. The Commissioner (D) denied the deduction because no physical injury had been done to their property.

Issue. May a casualty loss deduction be claimed without actual physical damage to the taxpayer's property?

Held. No. Commissioner's denial affirmed.

♦ Congress intended this deduction to be available only in cases involving actual physical damage to property. In this case, there was no actual damage to the property itself, and access was not blocked. Even if the value has been decreased, this type of hypothetical change in value cannot be accurately determined and is beyond what Congress had in mind.

3) **Lost property--**

Mary Frances Allen v. Commissioner, 16 T.C. 163 (1951).

Facts. Mary Frances Allen visited the New York Metropolitan Museum of Art. At the time, she was wearing a brooch, which disappeared and was never recovered. There was no proof of a theft, but she claimed a casualty loss deduction based on the theft of the brooch.

Issue. Does a taxpayer have the burden to present evidence, either direct or indirect, that leads to a reasonable inference that a loss was due to theft?

Held. Yes. Claim denied.

◆ The taxpayer has the burden of proof to present evidence that reasonably leads to the conclusion that the article was stolen. If reasonable inferences drawn from the evidence point to theft, the taxpayer wins. If the opposite is true, the taxpayer fails. And if the evidence does not point in either direction, the taxpayer still fails to carry the burden of proof.

◆ In this case, the taxpayer has not shown the nature of the clasp or whether she was jostled in a crowd (a usual occurrence during a theft). Thus, she has failed to carry the burden of proof.

Dissent.

◆ Evidence was that Allen was wearing the brooch at 4:30 in the museum. She mingled with a crowd of 5,000 people and discovered the brooch missing at 5:00, whereupon an unsuccessful search was conducted. If this evidence is true, there are only three possibilities: (i) the brooch was never found, (ii) it was found but not returned, and (iii) it was stolen. The first is highly unlikely, and the second amounts to theft when such a large and valuable object is involved under these circumstances.

◆ No matter what type of clasp it was, the evidence would only point to theft. If it were a safety clasp, then it must have been removed by a skillful thief since it could not have inadvertently fallen off. If it were a simple clasp, a thief could easily remove it. Hence, the majority's opinion can only be based on the assumption that Allen was not being candid.

———————

b. **Measuring the loss.** A taxpayer can deduct the lesser of (i) the adjusted basis of the property or (ii) the difference between the value of the property immediately before and immediately after the disaster (less $100). However, these losses are deductible only to the extent that total casualty and theft losses for the year exceed 10% of the adjusted gross income. It had been argued that because tax laws do not allow nonbusiness property to be depreciated, when such property is destroyed, the loss should be measured by its original cost. However, the Supreme Court has held that the loss is to be measured by the property's value at the time of the loss. [Helvering v. Owens, 305 U.S. 468 (1939)]

VII. DEFERRAL AND NONRECOGNITION OF INCOME AND DEDUCTIONS

A. DEFERRED REPORTING OF GAINS

1. **"Open Transaction" Doctrine.** The amount of gain or loss is determined by the difference between the amount realized on a disposition and the adjusted basis of the property relinquished. If the amount realized is unknown or uncertain, the gain or loss cannot be measured, and the transaction is an "open transaction." The regulations under I.R.C. section 1001 state that open transactions occur in only rare and extraordinary circumstances. It is the IRS's position that the fair market value of the amount realized can always be determined or reasonably estimated.

    a. **Timing and character of gain--**

Burnet v. Logan, 283 U.S. 404 (1931).

Facts. Logan (P) and others sold their stock in an iron company, which owned an interest in an iron ore mine. In return, P received cash plus an agreement that the buyer of the stock would pay P 60¢ for each ton of ore extracted from the mine. The Commissioner (D) ruled that each payment for extracted ore could be allocated between return of capital and taxable gain. D argued that the value of the future payments for the ore could be reasonably estimated. The court of appeals, however, ruled that it was impossible to determine the fair market value of the agreement. Therefore, P could allocate all payments to return-of-capital before recognizing any gain. D appeals.

Issue. In an open-ended transaction where the amount to be received is not determinable, can the seller recover his basis before recognizing any tax liability?

Held. Yes. Judgment affirmed.

♦ The transaction was not a closed one. The consideration for the sale was $2.2 million in cash and the promise of future money payments, contingent upon facts and circumstances not possible to foretell with any fair certainty. The promise was in no proper sense equivalent to cash and had no ascertainable fair market value.

Comment. All payments received under the "open transaction" approach of *Burnet v. Logan* are taxed as capital gains, after basis has been recovered. But if the contract can be valued and the transaction closed, an immediate gain or loss is computed. Moreover, if the taxpayer later recovers more than the value of the contract, the profit is ordinary income.

b. **Narrow application.** As a result, the "open transaction" approach is confined to unusual cases; the IRS prefers to value the purchaser's obligation if possible and "close" the transaction.

2. **Timing and Character of Gain in a Closed Transaction.**

a. **Transaction under I.R.C. section 453 election.** Section 453 allows taxpayers to defer income taxes until payments are received. It is intended to meet the problem faced by sellers of property in installments: they have to pay tax on their gain when the sale is made but do not yet have much cash from the sale. Under this method, the profit is prorated over the term of the payments. The Tax Reform Act of 1986 modified the installment sale rules. The installment method has been eliminated for (i) sales of publicly traded stocks and securities, and (ii) sales using revolving credit plans. The new rules modify other installment sales by treating a portion of the seller's outstanding debt obligations as amounts received on the installment contract.

1) **Computation.** To compute the gain that is recognizable each year, first the fraction of "gross profit" over the "total contract price" is computed. This fraction is applied to each future installment payment made to determine how much of the installment is gain to the seller.

2) **Losses.** The installment method cannot be used to spread a loss over the years of payment. It applies only to gains.

3) **Other installment sale rules.**

a) At least one payment must be received after the close of the taxable year in which the disposition occurs.

b) The installment sale rules automatically apply unless the taxpayer elects out of the rules.

c) If property is sold to a related party under the installment sale provisions and the related party makes a second disposition, the amount received by the second seller is treated as received by the first seller.

d) Recapture under I.R.C. sections 1245 and 1250 is recognized in the year of sale regardless of the amount received in such year.

e) I.R.C. section 453A treats a portion of the taxpayer's outstanding indebtedness as received in the year of sale. These special rules apply to sales of inventory type items, sales of real estate in the ordinary course of business, and sales of rental real estate in excess of $150,000.

b. **Related party sales—resale rule.** When a member of a family group makes an installment sale to a related person (first sale) who in turn sells within two years and before the installment payments are made in full (resale), the person who made the first sale must report the rest of the gain on her installment sale in the year that the related party made the resale, rather than as the installments are received by her, unless the resale and second disposition is one of the following:

1) A nonliquidating installment sale of stock to the issuing corporation;

2) An involuntary conversion if the first installment sale occurred before the threat or imminence of conversion;

3) A resale occurring after the death of the installment seller or related purchaser;

4) A case where it is established to the satisfaction of the IRS that neither disposition had tax avoidance as a principal purpose; or

5) A case where the second disposition is also an installment sale if the terms of the installment resale are equivalent or longer than those of the first installment sale.

c. **Disposition of installment obligations.** If the taxpayer has been using the installment method and sells or otherwise disposes of the obligation, the gain that was not previously taken into income is immediately recognized. This even applies to a gift of the receivable. However, if the taxpayer dies, the deferred gain is not recognized, and the estate or legatees are entitled to continue reporting the payments on the installment method.

B. ORIGINAL ISSUE DISCOUNT

The Original Issue Discount ("OID") rules are contained in I.R.C. sections 1271 to 1275. The intent of these sections is to insure that transactions reflect the time value of money. For example, if a transaction involving the sale of property does not reflect a market interest rate, such a rate will be imputed. These rules are applied to both cash- and accrual-basis taxpayers. The OID rules apply to the issuance of debt instruments as well as the sale of property. The OID rules require taxpayers to recognize OID income regardless of whether cash is received.

To the extent that the OID rules do not apply to the sale of property, I.R.C. section 483 may apply. I.R.C. section 483 requires a portion of each payment to be characterized as interest income. However, it does not require cash-basis taxpayers to recognize income without the receipt of cash.

C. DISALLOWANCE OF LOSSES

1. **Losses Between Related Taxpayers.** I.R.C. section 267 disallows deductions for expenses and losses between related parties. These include transactions between family members and between a corporation and a majority shareholder. The operation of section 267 is mandatory; loss is disallowed even if the sale was at arm's length and the price was fair. Since 1984, sales between spouses (including divorcing spouses) no longer give rise to recognized gain or loss.

   a. **Deduction disallowed--**

McWilliams v. Commissioner, 331 U.S. 694 (1947).

Facts. McWilliams (P) and his wife had independent estates, which P managed. P often sold securities from one estate to the other through the stock exchange. P claimed deductions when losses were sustained by one of the estates on various sales. The Commissioner (D) disallowed the loss deductions as occurring between family members. P argued that I.R.C. section 267(a)(1) applies only to intrafamily transfers and not to those administered through a public exchange. The Tax Court held for D, but the court of appeals reversed. D appeals.

Issue. Does section 267(a)(1), which disallows deductions for losses on transactions between family members, apply when a transaction involved a third party?

Held. Yes. Judgment affirmed.

♦ Even though these were bona fide sales through a public market, the end result is the same as if a transfer prohibited by section 267(a)(1) was effected. Transfers of property between family members do not generate losses since there is an identity of economic interest among all the family members. The introduction of a third party into the transaction does not change the result. The sales made by P fit within the evil that Congress sought to eliminate by enacting section 267(a)(1).

Comment. Although the seller is unable to claim a loss, the purchaser of the property is allowed to assume the seller's basis instead of his lower cost, but only if the purchaser later sells at a gain. For example, if A sells a tractor having a basis of $12,000 to her son B for $10,000, A cannot deduct the loss. However, when B later sells the tractor to a third party for $15,000, B will be allowed to use A's higher basis ($12,000) in computing his gain. B's gain in this case would be $3,000 instead of $5,000.

2. **Wash Sales.** Where a taxpayer sells stocks or securities and buys the same (or substantially identical) security within 30 days before or after the sale,

the transaction is dubbed a "wash sale" and is, in effect, ignored. I.R.C. section 1091 expressly provides that losses from wash sales are not deductible. The repurchased stock retains the same basis as the original stock (increased or decreased if the repurchase price was more or less than the sale price).

D. NONRECOGNITION PROVISIONS

Gain or loss on the sale or exchange of a capital asset is not always recognized by the taxpayer. I.R.C. sections 1031 through 1042 deal with the "tax-free exchanges." Under these provisions, the taxpayer need not claim a capital gain or loss. In most cases, the taxpayer assumes the basis of the previous owner of the asset. This allows the taxpayer to defer her gain until she finally sells the property.

1. **Exchanges of "Like Kind" Properties.** No gain or loss is recognized on an exchange when property held either for investment or for use in business is exchanged solely for property of like kind. [I.R.C. §1031(a)] The Tax Reform Act of 1986 requires that new property be identified within 45 days of the transaction. In addition, the acquisition of the new property must be completed within 180 days of the transaction.

   a. **What is an exchange?** In a "sale," property is transferred in exchange for money. In an "exchange," one thing is given for another. Where relatively small amounts of money are present, the transaction may be either a sale or an exchange, depending on the amount of cash and the nature of the transfer. The presence of a small amount of cash to adjust differences in value of the properties exchanged does not necessarily prevent the transaction from being considered an exchange. [Bloomington Coca-Cola Bottling Co. v. Commissioner, 189 F.2d 14 (7th Cir. 1951)]

   b. **"Like kind" defined--**

Commissioner v. Crichton, 122 F.2d 181 (5th Cir. 1941).

Facts. Crichton's (P's) children transferred their individual interests in an improved city lot worth $15,357 to P in exchange for an undivided one-fourth interest in oil, gas, and minerals lying under an unimproved country lot owned by P. The mineral rights had a cost basis of zero. The Commissioner (D) assessed a tax on the transaction on the ground that P had made a $15,357 capital gain. P alleged that under state law, the mineral rights were deemed real property, and alleged that the transaction was therefore an exchange of like property and tax exempt. The Board of Tax Appeals held for P, and the Commissioner appeals.

Issue. Is the exchange of improved real estate for mineral interests an exchange of "like kind" property?

Held. Yes. Judgment affirmed.

♦ As long as there is a transfer of like property, the transfer is deemed an exchange and is tax exempt. The basis of the transfers or the value of the property being transferred is immaterial. Both of the items transferred were real property. The fact that one was a fractional interest in surface land and the other was a mineral right does not render the exchange one of unlike properties.

Comment. "Like kind" refers to the general nature or character of the property—not to its grade or quality.

---

    c. **Coverage limited to property held for use.** I.R.C. section 1031 does not apply to stocks and bonds, nor does it apply to stock in trade, inventory, or other property held for sale in a trade or business. It covers only property held for *use*; *e.g.,* buildings, machinery, or fixtures.

    d. **Sale and leaseback at fair market value--**

Leslie Co. v. Commissioner, 539 F.2d 943 (3d Cir. 1976).

Facts. Leslie Company (P) decided to build a larger manufacturing plant but was unable to obtain financing. Prudential Insurance Company agreed to advance $2.4 million for the construction of the plant. After construction, P was to sell Prudential the plant for $2.4 million or its actual construction cost, whichever was less. P then would sign a 30-year lease with two 10-year options. The plant actually cost $3,187,000 to build. Under the contract terms, P "sold" the building to Prudential for $2.4 million, and a loss of $787,000 was reported from the "sale." The Commissioner (D) denied the loss, alleging that this was an exchange. The court found that the fair market value of the property was approximately $2.4 million and that the transaction was a sale with a concurrent condition requiring a lease. Since the sale was for the full market value of the plant, the lease had no capital value, and P was entitled to deduct the entire amount. D appeals.

Issue. When property is sold for its approximate fair market value, will the presence of a long-term leaseback render the transaction an exchange?

Held. No. Judgment affirmed.

♦ When the sale is for the fair market value of the property, the presence of a long-term leaseback will not render the transaction an exchange. Treasury Regulation section 1.1002(d) states that an exchange must involve the reciprocal transfer of property. However, if an asset is sold for an amount of money equal to its fair market value, the transaction is a "sale."

♦ There is no reason to consider the transaction in this case an exchange of a lease for property. The lease was merely a condition of sale. It had no separate value because P was still required by its terms to pay full and fair rental value. Valuation of the property is the key to such transactions. Since this transaction was a sale, loss may be taken on it.

---

e. **Three-cornered exchanges—Revenue Ruling 77-297.** A entered into an agreement to sell his ranch to B for $1,000. B agreed to put $100 into escrow, to assume $160 of debt, to execute a note in the amount of $540, and to pay $200 at closing. In addition, B promised to cooperate with A to effectuate a like kind exchange of properties if A should locate suitable property. A located suitable property owned by C. B purchased the property owned by C for cash and a note. B then exchanged the property purchased from C for the property owned by A. C allowed A to assume B's note owed to C and released B from the note. The escrow agent refunded the money B placed into escrow since the conditions of the escrow were never satisfied. The IRS ruled that this transaction qualifies as a like kind exchange under I.R.C. section 1031 for A.

2. **Involuntary Conversions.** I.R.C. section 1033 governs the taxability of a receipt of insurance proceeds or an eminent domain award from the involuntary conversion of a taxpayer's property. This section provides that if a taxpayer replaces the involuntarily converted property within two years after the end of the tax year of the receipt of the conversion proceeds with property "similar or related in service or use," gain on the proceeds will be taxed only to the extent that it exceeds the taxpayer's replacement cost.

a. **Partial condemnations--**

Harry G. Masser v. Commissioner, 30 T.C. 741 (1958).

Facts. Masser operated an interstate trucking company using two pieces of property across the street from each other as his terminal facility. One piece was involuntarily converted under threat of condemnation by the city. To continue the business on the one piece of land would have been very expensive. Therefore, Masser sold the second piece, and used the proceeds to purchase other suitable property in the same neighborhood. He claimed both lots as involuntary conversion. The Commissioner disallowed the claim and assessed a deficiency. Masser paid and brought suit for a refund.

Issue. When two lots are used in a business as an economic unit, if one of the lots is involuntarily converted, does this cause the other lot to also be involuntarily converted?

Held. Yes. Decision for taxpayer.

♦ In this case, the two pieces of property, practically adjacent to each other, were acquired for the same purpose and were being used as one economic unit. After one lot was involuntarily sold as a result of a threat of condemnation by the city, the continuation of the business on one piece of property was impractical. Using good business judgment, Masser sold the other piece of property and used the proceeds to purchase replacement property in the same area. In light of these circumstances, the transaction considered as a whole constitutes a conversion of one economic property unit.

---

b. Requirement that replacement property be similar or related in use--

---

Clifton Investment Co. v. Commissioner, 312 F.2d 719 (6th Cir. 1963), *cert. denied*, 373 U.S. 921 (1963).

Facts. Clifton Investment Company (P) was forced to sell an office building under threat of condemnation in New York. The money was reinvested in the purchase of a hotel. The Commissioner (D) assessed a deficiency tax on the proceeds from the sale of the office building on the ground that the replacement property was not similar or related in use. P's contention that the transaction was an involuntary conversion of property involving a like kind reinvestment that is tax exempt under I.R.C. section 1033 was rejected by the Tax Court. In doing so, the Tax Court applied the "functional" or "end use" test, which focuses upon the actual physical end use by the taxpayer, to determine whether section 1033 treatment should be granted. P appeals.

Issue. Are two pieces of investment property that both produce rental income to the taxpayer substantially similar or related in service or use under section 1033?

Held. No. Judgment affirmed.

♦ The "functional" test applied by the Tax Court, however, is not broad enough to cover the case of a holder of investment property who replaces it with other investment property. Congress intended to grant tax-exempt treatment to investors who are subject to an involuntary conversion requiring a reinvestment of their funds, but did not intend to allow such treatment when the funds are used to venture into new areas of business. The reinvestment must be in substantially similar property.

♦ The question herein is whether a hotel is the substantial equivalent of an office building. All relevant factors, including management, nature of services, and number of employees, must be considered. Here, whereas P managed the office building itself, a professional management company was needed for the hotel. The office building had two employees; the hotel had 130 to 140 employees. The services offered were different, as were the uses of the building. Under these circumstances, the hotel was not a substantial equivalent of the office building, and section 1033 treatment is denied.

Concurrence. I think the investment character of the properties involved should be given more consideration.

Comment. Note that the requirement that the replacement property be "similar or related in use" under section 1033 is much stricter than the like kind test under section 1031.

---

    c.   **Election.** Under I.R.C. section 1033, a taxpayer can recognize the gain if she wants to. The section is elective. In addition, the section applies only to gains. Losses are deductible immediately.

    d.   **Special rule for business real property.** A special rule provides that as to condemnations of business real property (or sales of such property under threat of condemnation), no gain is recognized if the proceeds are reinvested in "like kind" property, whether or not "similar or related in service or use" to the property condemned. Thus, the more generous test of I.R.C. section 1031 is used rather than the stricter section 1033 test. Moreover, three years is allowed as the replacement period instead of the usual two.

    e.   **Revenue rulings—similar or related in service or use.**

        1)   **Revenue Ruling 76-319.** The IRS ruled that proceeds from the condemnation of a bowling center used to construct a billiard center did not qualify under I.R.C. section 1033.

        2)   **Revenue Ruling 67-254.** The IRS ruled that condemnation proceeds used to rearrange existing plant facilities and build new facilities on land already owned qualified as property similar or related in service or use.

        3)   **Revenue Ruling 71-41.** The IRS ruled that proceeds from the condemnation of a rental warehouse used to build a gas station that was rented qualified under I.R.C. section 1033.

3.   **Other Nonrecognition Provisions.**

    a.   **Mortgage repossessions.** Under I.R.C. section 1038, sellers of property who foreclose on such property only recognize gain on the foreclosure to the extent that money or other property received exceeds the amount of gain already recognized. The seller is required to restore any prior bad-debt deductions taken with respect to such property.

b. **Gain on sale of federally assisted low-income housing projects.** I.R.C. section 1039 provides that the seller of a federally assisted low-income housing project can elect not to recognize gain if (i) she sells to tenants or a tenant co-op, and (ii) she reinvests in similar property within a limited time.

c. **Bequests.** If an executor satisfies a pecuniary bequest with appreciated property, the estate does not recognize gain on the transfer.

1) **Exception—recognition on difference in value.** Gain is recognized to the extent that the value of the property on the date of transfer is greater than its value for estate tax purposes.

2) **Trusts.** The same rule applies to transfers of property by a trust, by reason of the death of a decedent, to satisfy an obligation to pay the beneficiary a specific sum.

3) **Basis.** The basis to the recipient is the same as the basis immediately before the exchange, increased by any gain recognized on the transfer.

VIII. CONVERTING TAXABLE INCOME INTO TAX LIABILITY

A. CLASSIFICATION OF TAXPAYER

1. **Four Rate Tables.** There are four separate progressive rate tables, each applicable to certain types of individuals. The tables are different with respect to brackets. However, the same basic 10%, 15%, 25%, 28%, 33%, and 35% tax rates are used.

   a. **Married individuals filing joint returns.** This rate table splits the income of the spouses equally between them. This is especially helpful if only one spouse earns all the income. Surviving spouses who for the two years following the year of their spouse's death do not remarry but do maintain certain dependents in their home are also accorded joint-filing status.

   b. **Heads of households.** Heads of households are unmarried persons who are required to maintain a household for the benefit of other individuals. These taxpayers are afforded one-half of the income-splitting relief given to the married taxpayer filing a joint return.

   c. **Unmarried individuals.** A single taxpayer is taxed at rates above those for married couples with similar income.

   d. **Married individuals filing separate returns.** These taxpayers pay the highest tax of all. The rates in this table also apply to estates and trusts.

2. **Historical Background and Policy Considerations.** Originally, all individuals were taxed under a single set of tax rates. In 1930, however, the Supreme Court held that in community property states, married individuals could split their income between them (and thus lower their combined tax liability). In response, many states enacted community property statutes. Partly to head off this trend, Congress passed a provision for filing joint returns. Since 1948, married couples have been allowed to split their income as if each spouse had earned one-half of the total. The 1948 Act gave married individuals an advantage over single taxpayers, no two of whom could split their incomes to lower their tax rates. In response to this, in 1969, Congress enacted a lower single-taxpayer rate schedule. Thus, a single taxpayer was taxed at a rate below that of a married taxpayer with a similar income. This compromise brought complaints from both sides. Single taxpayers bemoaned the income splitting afforded married taxpayers, while the latter group bemoaned the lower rates afforded single taxpayers.

B. CREDITS AGAINST TAX

After the amount of tax has been determined, as provided above, the taxpayer may be entitled to certain credits. These reduce the actual tax payable on a dollar-for-dollar basis.

1. **Credit for Taxes Withheld and Prepaid.** The taxpayer is entitled to a credit against taxes payable for all sums withheld from his wages for payment of taxes and for all amounts prepaid in connection with declarations of estimated tax. This credit and the earned income credit (*see infra*) are refundable; *i.e.,* they not only reduce tax but may also generate a refund. The other credits do not generate a refund if they exceed the amount of tax computed.

2. **Foreign Tax Credit.** In lieu of a deduction from income, the taxpayer may elect to take as a credit against tax the amount of income, excess profits, and similar taxes paid or accrued during the year to foreign countries or possessions of the United States. The amount of the credit is limited to that proportion of the tax that the taxable income from sources within the foreign country bears to the entire taxable income of the individual. Note that the taxpayer has the option to treat foreign taxes as a credit or a deduction from gross income, whichever is the most advantageous to him.

3. **Credit for the Elderly.** Taxpayers who are 65 or over receive a credit of 15% of their "section 22 amount."

   a. **"Section 22 amount."** This is $5,000 for a single individual, $7,500 in case of a joint return where both spouses are eligible, or $3,750 in the case of a married person filing a separate return.

   b. **Reductions from "section 22 amount."** The taxpayer must reduce the "section 22 amount" by Social Security received or other amounts excluded from gross income. (The "section 22 amount" does not have to be reduced by life insurance, annuities, compensation for personal injuries or sickness, or amounts received under accident or health plans.)

      1) Moreover, if adjusted gross income exceeds $7,500, the "section 22 amount" is further reduced by one-half of the excess over $7,500. (This figure is $10,000 in case of a joint return, and $5,000 in case of a married person filing a separate return.)

4. **Qualified Adoption Credit.** I.R.C. section 23 allows a $10,000 child credit for qualified adoption expenses.

5. **Child Credit.** I.R.C. section 24 provides a credit of $1,000 for each qualifying child for low- and middle-income taxpayers.

6. **Investment Credit.** Prior to the Tax Reform Act of 1986, taxpayers were entitled to a credit in an amount up to 10% of the investment that the taxpayer

had made during the year in certain types of depreciable property. This credit is no longer available.

7. **Targeted Jobs Credit.** I.R.C. section 51 allows for a credit based on qualifying wages paid to qualifying members of a targeted group.

8. **Child-Care Expense Credit.** Traditionally, the courts permitted no business expense deduction for child-care costs. Eventually, however, Congress provided a limited deduction, then broadened the deduction, and finally switched to a credit.

   a. **Amount and definition.** A credit is allowed for "employment-related expenses" if there is a "qualifying individual in the home." Employment-related expenses are those for household services and for care of a qualifying individual—but only if incurred to enable the taxpayer to be gainfully employed. A "qualifying individual" is a dependent under age 13 (for whom the taxpayer is entitled to claim the exemption), or a dependent (of the taxpayer or taxpayer's spouse) who is unable to care for himself.

   b. **Dollar limitation.** The child-care credit is 35% of eligible expenses for taxpayers with taxable income of $15,000 or less. The credit is reduced by one percentage point for each $2,000 (or fraction thereof) of income above $15,000. The maximum amount of expenditures with respect to which a credit can be taken is $3,000 (for one dependent) and $6,000 (for two or more dependents). Expenses for out-of-home, noninstitutional care of a disabled spouse or dependent are eligible for the credit, but expenditures at a child-care center not in compliance with state or local regulations are not eligible for the credit. Finally, amounts provided by an employer under a nondiscriminatory child-care plan are not included in the employee's income.

   c. **Divorced parents included.** Even if a custodial parent is not entitled to claim an exemption, he can take the child-care credit.

9. **Earned Income Credit.** Low-income taxpayers are allowed a credit against their income tax liability based upon a percentage of their earned income. The credit is phased out as their income exceeds certain levels. This credit can exceed the amount of taxes paid and is designed to reward low-income individuals for working.

C. ALTERNATIVE MINIMUM TAX

Once taxable income is calculated by reducing gross income and adjusted gross income by the deductions to which the taxpayer is entitled (including deductions arising from capital gains and losses), the percentage tax rates under I.R.C. section 1 are applied to determine the tax payable. However, an "alternative minimum tax" may apply. [I.R.C. §55]

1. **"Alternative Minimum Tax."** The Alternative Minimum Tax ("AMT") is a tax that is imposed if a taxpayer's regular tax liability is reduced below the AMT level. The objective of the AMT is to impose a minimum level of tax on taxpayers who shelter their regular tax liability by using preference items. The tax is based on a broader definition of income and is imposed at 26% and 28% rates on Alternative Minimum Taxable Income ("AMTI").

   a. **Computation.** First compute AMTI. The term "AMTI" means regular taxable income determined with adjustments under I.R.C. sections 56 and 58 and increased by tax preference items described in I.R.C. section 57. Then subtract an exemption (as of 2006, $62,550 on a joint return, $42,500 for a single person, $31,275 for the single return of a married person). The exemption amounts are phased out when the taxpayer's AMTI exceeds certain levels. The balance is taxable at the rates of 26% and 28%. The taxpayer then pays either his regular tax or the AMT, whichever is the greater amount.

   b. **Adjustments under I.R.C. section 56.** The adjustments required to compute AMTI are as follows:

      1) A taxpayer must use 150% declining balance depreciation on nonreal business property (such as trucks or machines);

      2) No deductions are allowed for any miscellaneous itemized deductions;

      3) Medical deductions are limited to a floor of 10% of AGI rather than 7.5%;

      4) The deduction from AGI for state, local, and foreign taxes (such as income tax and real property tax) is not allowed for AMT purposes;

      5) Standard deductions and personal exemptions are not available under the AMT, but the overall limit on itemized deductions that applies on the regular tax does not apply to the AMT;

      6) Long-term contracts must reflect the percentage of completion method of accounting; and

      7) Only interest incurred in acquiring, constructing, or improving a qualified residence is deductible under the AMT.

   c. **Tax preferences.** The tax preferences subject to the alternative minimum tax include:

      1) Certain tax-exempt interest;

2) Financial institution bad-debt reserves;

3) Pre-1987 ACRS deductions on leased personal property in excess of a figure computed using straight-line depreciation over a useful life of five years (for three-year property) and eight years (for five-year property);

4) Pre-1987 ACRS deductions on 15-year real property (whether or not leased) in excess of straight-line depreciation;

5) The bargain element of an incentive stock option when exercised;

6) The excess of percentage depletion over adjusted basis of a mine or oil and gas well;

7) The gain portion of charitable contributions of appreciated property; and

8) Intangible drilling costs on oil and gas wells (less the amount of such costs that would be recovered through straight-line depreciation) in excess of net income from oil and gas.

d. **Credits.** A credit will be allowed to reduce regular tax for AMT that is paid attributable to timing items. "Timing items" are items that are included in AMTI currently but will be in regular taxable income in future years.

e. **Applies to taxpayers with no tax preferences--**

Klaasen v. Commissioner, 76 T.C.M. 20 (1998).

Facts. The Klaasens' (Ps') religious beliefs encouraged them to have a large family. In 1994, Ps rightfully claimed 12 exemptions, 10 for their children and 2 for themselves. Ps itemized their deductions, claiming $4,767.13 in medical deductions and $3,263.56 in state and local taxes. Ps did not complete the alternative minimum tax form with their 1994 return. The Commissioner (D) sent a notice of deficiency for $1,085.43 in minimum taxes for 1994. Ps claim that since they do not have any tax preference items within the meaning of section 57, they are not subject to minimum tax. In addition, Ps claim that the minimum tax violates various constitutional rights, particularly religious freedom.

Issue. Does the alternative minimum tax apply to taxpayers who do not have any tax preference items?

Held. Yes. Judgment affirmed.

♦ The statute in question clearly defined the calculation to determine alternative minimum tax and left no room for interpretation. If Congress had intended to tax only preferences, it would have defined "alternative minimum taxable income" differently.

♦   Furthermore, the alternative minimum tax does not unconstitutionally inhibit free exercise of religion.

Comment. Note that the AMT exemption is not indexed for inflation. Unless the tax is modified by Congress, more and more taxpayers will be subject to AMT in the future.

IX. FEDERAL TAX PROCEDURE AND PROFESSIONAL RESPONSIBILITY

A. OVERVIEW OF FEDERAL TAX PROCEDURE

1.   **Filing the Tax Return.** The federal tax system requires taxpayers to make their own determination of their tax liability. Most individuals file returns (Form 1040, 1040A, or 1040EZ) on a calendar year basis and must file by April 15 of the following year. However, in many cases, the taxpayer's liability has already been paid by his employer by withholding a portion of the taxpayer's income and depositing the amount with the government. At year end, the employer is required to give all employees a statement of their individual wages withheld and paid (Form W-2). Individuals who receive their income from other sources such as interest or dividends are not subject to withholding laws. Therefore, they must estimate their taxable income and pay their estimated tax liability in quarterly installments. Individuals who do not comply may be subject to interest and penalty charges.

2.   **IRS Review of Returns.** The review of taxpayers' returns begins with a check for mathematical errors. All returns are then subjected to a computer screening process, which identifies returns that have a likelihood of audit adjustments. This process tends to select corporate tax returns and individual income tax returns with high income, large deductions, or some other deviation from the statistical norm. The specific criteria that govern whether a return will be audited are carefully guarded by the IRS. Generally, the IRS has only three years from the time the return is filed to assess additional tax.

3.   **Audit and Administrative Appeals Procedure.** An audit can take one of three forms. In a "correspondence audit," the taxpayer is asked to mail specific information to the IRS. An "office audit" requires the taxpayer to appear at the district director's office. In a "field audit," the IRS official examines the taxpayer's books and materials at her place of business. If the audit is conducted by a "special agent" rather than a "revenue agent," a civil penalty assessment or criminal charge may be in the offing. If the taxpayer and agent cannot resolve their differences, the taxpayer is given a "30-day letter," which gives her that amount of time to appeal to the district director. If the taxpayer chooses, she may disregard the 30-day letter and petition the Tax Court.

   a.   **Administrative reviews.** The district and appellate offices offer an informal appeal process whereby the taxpayer, with or without counsel, is given opportunity to air her side of the case. Most cases heard here are resolved. If a dispute remains, the taxpayer may take her appeal from the district office to the appellate division. If the administrative procedure is exhausted without resolution, the taxpayer has three avenues of judicial recourse.

      b.   **Judicial review.** An appeal is usually filed with the Tax Court, which stays any tax assessment. A review can also be brought, after payment of the disputed deficiency, to the district court or the United States Claims Court.

    4.   **Collection of Tax.** After proper assessment, the government has six years to collect the tax. If a taxpayer can establish hardship, the IRS has the authority to let her delay in her payment of tax or even compromise the amount of the tax liability. If no extension or compromise is given, the IRS uses the collection provisions discussed below.

      a.   **Federal tax lien.** A lien for federal taxes arises when a taxpayer's liability has been assessed. Such lien attaches to all of the property the taxpayer holds or will acquire. However, certain classes of persons have priority over an income tax lien. Those include purchasers, secured creditors, mortgagees, pledgees, and judgment lien creditors. This is an area where tax law is intertwined with other areas of the law, particularly the Uniform Commercial Code.

      b.   **Jeopardy assessments.** If a revenue agent believes for any reason that a delay would "jeopardize" the collection of a tax, the agent does not have to wait for the taxpayer to file her tax return to take action. The agent can declare the taxpayer's tax year ended, determine what tax is due, and demand immediate payment. If payment is not forthcoming, the agent may seize the taxpayer's savings, wages, and property. The jeopardy assessment is a useful tool to stop criminals from skipping the country without paying their taxes or from hiding their assets before an audit can be conducted. However, many taxpayers have sharply criticized this procedure. They contend that the immediate seizure of property is done without due process since a taxpayer is not given notice or a hearing. Others contend that the IRS has a penchant for assessing far in excess of what they truly believe is owed. Also, an innocent taxpayer may be left without sufficient funds to contest the assessment and may be forced to go through a lengthy court battle to reacquire her property.

B. TAX FRAUD

Special agents of the Intelligence Division of the IRS will be assigned when a tax fraud investigation is approved. It is important that the taxpayer's representative recognize at the earliest possible time that a tax fraud investigation is being conducted. Generally, this will be apparent from the way an audit is being conducted. When the audit is complete, the special agent, if she recommends prosecution, will do so in a detailed report, which is reviewed by the special agent's group chief. This report, if approved by the Intelligence Division, is then forwarded to the Regional Counsel's office where a determination is made (i) whether the taxpayer is in fact guilty of tax evasion and (ii) whether there is a reasonable chance of securing a conviction. This report is then forwarded to the Justice Department, where a final determination is made whether to prosecute. If prosecution is recommended, then the case is forwarded to the appropriate United States Attorney's office, usually with instructions to secure an indictment.

1. **Examination of Witnesses and Records.** I.R.C. section 7602 authorizes the IRS to examine books, papers, or records and take testimony from witnesses. Search warrants, subpoenas, and summonses are not, however, self-executing and must be enforced in court.

2. **Resisting Summons.** The court will not enforce a summons issued to harass the taxpayer or to create pressure to settle a collateral dispute, or where the leads to the records in question were obtained in an unlawful search and seizure.

3. **Additional Tax Must Be Due.** Ordinarily, proof of a tax deficiency is an essential element in proving tax fraud.

4. **Meeting the Special Agent.** Whenever the taxpayer makes statements to the special agent, they are invariably damaging. Thus, in all but the most routine audits, communications with the IRS should be through the taxpayer's representative. In fact, it is best if the taxpayer is not even present at meetings or conferences.

5. **Constitutional Protection.** The Fifth Amendment privilege against self-incrimination applies to an individual's oral testimony and written communications, including personal business and tax records. However, the privilege does not apply to records of a corporation or partnership.

6. **Cooperation by the Taxpayer.** Any doubts about cooperation with the IRS should be resolved against cooperation.

C. REFUND AND DEFICIENCY PROCEDURES

As outlined above, the taxpayer may either pay the tax and file a claim for refund in the United States District Court or the Court of Claims or make no tax payment and petition the Tax Court. The entire amount of the deficiency must be paid in order to maintain a refund suit.

1. **Additions to Tax.** If the taxpayer loses a deficiency controversy, she may be required to pay interest, penalties, and additional penalties for negligence or fraud.

2. **Joint and Several Liability.** Husbands and wives are jointly and severally liable on joint income tax returns. However, I.R.C. section 6013(e), known as the "innocent spouse rule," provides some measure of relief.

3. **Small Tax Cases.** An estate, gift, or income tax case that does not involve over $1,500 can be handled as a "small" tax case under simplified rules of procedure. Decisions are not subject to appeal and do not serve as precedent.

D. PROFESSIONAL RESPONSIBILITY AND CIRCULAR 230

Tax lawyers, like all lawyers, must balance the responsibilities of advocating for their clients with their obligations to the legal system. There are special ethical standards that govern practice before the IRS. Circular 230, contained in Title 31 of the Code of Federal Regulations, sets out the duties and restrictions for attorneys and other professionals practicing before the IRS, as well as the sanctions against those who violate the regulations. Among other matters, Circular 230 addresses the exercise of due diligence, the strict requirements for tax opinions, disclosure of information requested by the IRS, tax shelter reporting obligations, and procedures to ensure compliance.

TABLE OF CASES
(Page numbers of briefed cases in bold)